Recession Cures

Kevin Trudeau

A Personal Note from the Author

Research for this book was conducted for many months - even before economists were using the term "recession". From the day I started writing until the book went to print, an election changed the President and many members of Congress, there were changes in laws and legislation, and there were many changes in the economic situation in America. Banks and insurance companies have been changing their policies. Prices have changed too!

We were constantly updating and revising the information to keep it as accurate and relevant as possible. But we didn't want to hold off on bringing you the valuable advice, tips, and facts that could change your financial situation. So I offer a personal apology if some of the information has changed, and I caution that you should make sure to confirm that there have been no changes in law or updates in policies.

The bottom line is that regardless of the changes in policies and law, and despite all the money that the U.S. government has been giving to banks and major companies, the economic reality is that the average American is suffering. You need to know how to improve your financial status. And this book should help you do that.

Over the past few years, there have been many friends, colleagues, and advisors who have helped me identify the foremost problems facing us, and who have stood behind me in my efforts to find the best solutions to resolve those problems. When the recession began, they were unanimous in recommending a comprehensive guide to surviving the recession. Their suggestions and adice were thoroughly researched and compiled, and are presented to you in the pages of this book.

A tremendous thank you to all who helped and supported me through this valuable and important project. Because of you, this book has changed my life. I hope it will have the same positive effect on the readers.

Table of Contents

1

What is A Recession... And Are We In One?

The financial news on TV and in the newspapers has been depressing for months, but it really became frightening when economists began using the word "recession". For a while, they were saying that we might be headed for a recession, or maybe there are symptoms of one. Why did it take so long for economists to actually begin calling it a recession?

"Recession" has a specific, technical definition. In economics, this term usually means a situation in which a country's gross domestic product (GDP) sustains a negative growth factor for two consecutive quarters (six months). Some economists say that a recession occurs when the GDP's natural growth rate is less than the average of 2%. Many government agencies define a recession as a long-term decline in economic growth and, in fact, might not officially announce a recession until we have been in one for six months or even longer. Typically, an economic recession lasts for approximately one year, although this time they are predicting that it could be longer.

Right now, we are experiencing an economic downturn that is aggravated by American companies outsourcing their labor needs overseas. The result? U.S. employers are cutting wages; oil prices are rising; the government is taking more money out of your pay check in the form of taxes or fees; and many well-known companies are closing their doors altogether. And if the U.S. economy is in a state of recession, you're at risk of, or already experiencing, a personal recession.

Many U.S. economists agree that we are facing the worst economic times since the Great Depression. Shortly before he took office, it was frightening to hear President Barack Obama on *Meet the Press,* talking about how bad things are. In fact, he mentioned a number of times that "Things are going to get worse before they get better." And, indeed, they have.

"Things getting worse before they get better" are tough words to swallow when we are already facing the worst unemployment numbers in years. At the end of 2008, a *Washington Post* headline read, "Monthly loss of jobs worst in 34 years". Over 500,000 jobs were lost in December 2008, and they were telling us that things were still going to get worse?

Whether you personally feel a direct or indirect impact, the recession affects everyone in one way or another. It has become a dangerous snowball that began with the weeding out of weak or over-exposed businesses. As the recession grows, it can affect your job and put at risk the things you need most.

Many businesses are working on a mode of "anything but business as usual", with their monthly revenue stream experiencing a drastic setback. Since those businesses are selling lower volumes of services or fewer products and subsequently losing profits, they are forced to cut costs themselves or increase their prices.

This, of course, has some effect on an increasing inflation rate, which is not good for anyone. Less money coupled with higher costs means dangerous times.

As a result of higher costs and lower profits, businesses have to make serious decisions. Because of the credit crisis, they can't get approved for more loans or credit from the bank. As a result, they may be unable to write your paycheck, and they may have to start laying off employees or completely close their doors.

That, of course, worsens the condition for those who are already strapped for cash, which means more belt-tightening or increased credit card debt on a personal level. We see that hurting businesses funnels down to affect families and individuals.

Hopefully you and your family are not badly touched by the recession directly. Perhaps you will experience indirect exposure when you look at your community and see the impact on the lives of those around you. How many people do you know that have lost their jobs? How many neighbors have children, parents or other family members coming to live with them? How many boarded up homes do you pass on your way to work?

These are troubled times for all of us, forcing us to think strategically and have a "what if" plan of action. It's easy to think "It won't happen to me. I have a great job, a stable income, and I'm smarter than that."

There are some who are going to be prepared, and some who are going to have their worlds rocked. Later in the book I will tell you how to prepare for a personal recession.

2

Symptoms of Recession

In 1980, Ronald Reagan famously asked the American people, "Are you better off than you were four years ago?" Today, with the Bush administration having recently come to a close, I believe it is worth asking whether the last eight years of government policies have left Americans better off than they were ten years ago.

A variety of metrics can be used to judge this question and assess what the past eight years of government policies have wrought. The picture painted here is clear: from job growth to debt, and from income disparity to national poverty indices, the conservative approach of putting big corporations and the wealthy ahead of the middle class has failed to create prosperity that can be shared by all Americans.

Job growth has lagged behind population growth. The number of new jobs rose by just over 2% between 2001-2008, compared to more than a 21% increase between 1993-2001. Middle-class incomes have dropped. The typical American household earned 0.6% less in 2007 in real terms than they did in 2000. Income disparity has grown. In fact, the income disparity levels today show a striking resemblance to 1928, the beginning of the Great Depression. Total household income grew by $863 billion from 2002-2006, of which 72% ($626 billion) went to the top 1% of wealthiest Americans, while only 5% (or $41 billion) went to the bottom 90%. The misery index has also increased. The misery index - the sum of the unemployment rate and the rate of inflation - has risen from 7.93% in January 2001 to 11.04% in September 2008.

More Americans today are living without insurance. The number of people without health insurance has grown by 12%, rising from 38 million in 2000 to 46 million in 2008. This is because the cost of insurance has skyrocketed. The average cost of an employer-provided family premium jumped from $6,800 in 2000 to $12,700 in 2008.

The number of children living in poverty has risen by 15%, from 11.6 million in 2000 to 13.3 million in 2007. The number of families living in poverty has more than doubled, going from 6.4 million in 2000 to 13.3 million in 2007.

So are we better off today than we were eight years ago? Did eight years of unchecked government policies serve you and your family well? What does this all mean to us now, in this recession?

3

What Happened to the Middle Class?

When I was growing up, my parents and their friends had good blue-collar jobs. They were firemen, policemen, school teachers, and factory workers. When they were in their early twenties, they were able to buy houses, or buy land and build their own houses, without putting themselves deep into debt. Can anyone do that now?

The economic life of Middle America is stagnating and growing at the same time. The statistics are very deceiving. Although incomes have risen, expenses have too. Income growth over the past three decades bypassed American's middle class and mostly benefited the rich. Middle-class household incomes increased little, wages increased even less, and rising expenses drove families into debt. However, over the past thirty years, income per person almost doubled, people are healthier and living longer, and the variety, quantity and quality of goods and services being consumed are greater than ever.

How could it be that incomes rose so much, but people have not become more prosperous? Hourly compensation increased more than hourly wages. That means that although the gross wages on your paycheck may have increased, your net wages did not. Non-wage benefits grew rapidly, and adjustments were made for inflation. The hourly pay of middle Americans rose by almost 30% from 1975 to 2005 due to price inflation compensation.

Median household income adjusted for inflation only increased 18% over the past 30 years, according to the U.S. Census Bureau. In contrast, data from the Bureau of Economic Analysis indicate that income per person has risen 80%. This discrepancy exists because the rich reaped most of the benefits of economic growth over this period, while middle-income households gained less. It's no wonder that America's middle class has less buying power then they used to have, but they are expected to maintain a higher standard of living than ever before.

4

What You Need to Buy Costs More?

Have you noticed that today everything - all of the basic things you need to buy in order to live - costs more? From food to transportation to entertainment, prices have risen. Why? The unexpected answer is oil. The cost of oil determines the price of almost every other commodity that we buy. Oil, in the forms of gasoline, crude oil, and plastics, is a crucial part of production in almost every industry, including farming, manufacturing, and retail sales.

Gasoline costs about a dollar more per gallon today than it did a year ago. If it stays that way for a full year, a driver who drives 15,000 miles at 20 miles per gallon would spend an additional $750 a year. That would bring the average driver's total annual gasoline cost to $3,000.

Changing gas prices have probably already caused you to change your lifestyle in order to save money. You may have altered the way you commute to work. You probably have reconsidered vacation plans, cut back on what you spend on hobbies or recreation, and felt the resulting tension of higher gas prices at home. Sixty percent of employees have less discretionary income, and forty-five percent have to pay off debts slowly or not at all. Another twenty-six percent are not able to pay for the "basics", such as food or utilities like heat or air conditioning.

Many people think that they are simply unable to get ahead due to the price of gas and oil. They're wrong - it is only a perception, and later in the book I will show you the steps to getting ahead in this oil-driven economy.

Do you feel shocked when you pay $4-a-gallon for gas? It's not only the price at the pump that affects your income; less obvious damage to our paychecks is starting to trickle in from a hidden flood of oil-fueled price increases. Oil is used for every part of the economy - whether in the form of fuel used to transport food to the supermarket for sale or the crude oil used to create a plastic milk jug. When prices rise at the oil well, consumers eventually pay for it at every level of living.

Many consumer products are made from petroleum: For example, tires are 62% petroleum, a vacuum cleaner is 30% petroleum, and lipstick is 100% petroleum. Even paper owes about a quarter of the cost of its materials to oil. Consider a plastic bottle of shampoo. Aside from the water, all of the other ingredients come from oil-based products, including the surfactants and emulsifiers. The bottle is high-density polycarbonate, and the cap is made of another plastic. The label is made from paper and plastic resin. The ink on the label is a petroleum product. Likewise with the glue on the back of the label!

Economists say they can't completely predict the overall effect of oil prices on consumers, in part because other costs, such as labor, also affect how much things cost. However, the average family in the U.S. spent about $19,000 on consumer goods in 2006, so a relatively modest increase in prices across the board would definitely compound their expenditures.

Price increases that are linked to the cost of oil were recently announced by many companies, including some you may be familiar with: Dow Chemical, Huntsman Chemical, Kimberly-Clark, and Bridgestone Tire. That means the consumer goods you buy in the supermarket, drug store, and hardware store will continue to cost you more. If you reduce what you spend on oil products like gasoline and plastics, you can fight back against the recession. Later in the book, I will give you many concrete suggestions for cutting the cost of oil and gasoline in your life.

5

Jobs Are Moving Overseas

One of the biggest killers of good-paying American jobs is the off-shore shift of labor. CEOs hire software engineers, technical support staff, and credit card bill collectors located overseas, exploiting the low wages in poor nations. U.S. workers have been facing this serious threat for the past few years, with highly educated technology experts and service professionals increasingly having to compete against legions of college graduates in India, China, and the Philippines who are willing to work twice as hard for one-fifth the pay.

Many Americans have grounds to be very afraid of losing their jobs to outsourcing. Do you have friends who have been laid off recently? If they were replaced, it is more than likely that their jobs were outsourced overseas as an effort by their employer to stay afloat in this economy. The prime motive of most CEOs who opt to send labor offshore has been to take advantage of the "labor arbitrage", that huge wage gap between industrialized and developing nations. Today, millions of low-cost financial analysts, engineers, architects, and consumer marketers living outside of the United States are readily available to work for American companies via the Internet or phone

Big outsourcing deals are often accompanied by big layoffs. Don't fear, though; you can still find ways to make money in the United States. I'll show you the twelve steps of surviving the recession later in the book.

6

Rising Credit Card Debt

I'm sure you have heard the expression "sub-prime meltdown". Essentially, American banks recklessly lent money to people who bought homes they could not afford. This resulted in homeowners defaulting on close to $900 billion in mortgage loans that they could not pay for, which put banks out of business and sparked a domino-effect credit crisis.

Even if you do not have a mortgage, this meltdown affects you. In 2008, banks reported their worst quarterly results since 2001, and concerns about rising credit card delinquencies were heard alongside sub-prime woes. Initially, Citigroup reported a 57% decline in earnings, attributing part of its losses to consumer credit costs, and said it would put aside $2.24 billion in loan-loss reserves to cover future defaults. Other major financial institutions like American Express and Bank of America are preparing for disaster. The reality is that the $915 billion in U.S. credit card debt may explode as we witness it.

Credit card holders are maxing out the balances on their cards, or doing risky things like taking cash advances on those cards for the first time - behavior that can bring debt trouble. Experts anticipate that credit card delinquencies will rise as consumers, who have until now used home-equity lines of credit to pay off their balances, start racking up higher credit card debt. When housing prices were rising, consumers were able to tap the escalating values of their homes to keep borrowing. Without home-equity credit, consumers will now have a hard time paying off their credit card debt.

This matters to the economy because credit card debt is resold as packages of securities on the financial markets. Rising delinquencies not only would hurtthe banks involved, but the securities backed by the credit card receivables. As consumers default on their payments, those securities will lose value. This will cause bank and portfolio losses in hedge funds, pension funds and financial institutions, potentially wreaking havoc on the economy, just like the sub-prime crisis already has.

Most credit-card debt is unsecured, meaning consumers don't have to give a deposit when they open accounts. With mortgages, some banks can fall back on both down-payments and the ability to sell the property. With credit card delinquency, if someone stops making monthly payments and the account goes into default, the credit card company has no money to claim from the bad account. A default means a total loss for the bank. Just because a credit card is being marketed to you does not mean that it is good for you or good for the economy. In fact, it could get you into deep, unsecured debt, and help cause America's banks to collapse.

These troubles may sound familiar: Borrowers falling behind on their payments. Defaults rising. Loans going bad. Investors losing all their money. This isn't just the story of mortgages gone bad. The next nightmare is the $950 billion worth of outstanding credit-card debt, much of it toxic to the whole financial sector.

The credit-card crisis potentially affects more people than the sub-prime mortgage crisis because borrowers with low credit scores account for roughly thirty percent of outstanding credit-card debt, compared with eleven percent of mortgage debt. Credit-card losses are already taking a toll on lenders. To compensate, many firms are jacking up interest rates. Even if you are a responsible credit-card user, higher interest rates will cost you money. If you miss a single payment, you can expect your credit card company to charge you interest rates of up to thirty percent.

If you want to recession-proof yourself, you must free yourself from interest-based debt. Later in the book, I will give you great advice for reducing your credit card dependency. You can finally free yourself from the burden of debt!

7

Preparing for Retirement

Regardless of your age, you must plan ahead and save for your retirement. Social security and pensions will probably not exist when you retire, so you need to start preparing to depend on yourself. I know that saving is hard during a recession but, as you will read below, there are many reasons why it is important to prepare early for retirement. You can avoid these common myths:

• Some people, including women, continue to believe that only men retire. This misconception ignores the career women who have the same retirement adjustment problems that men have. Also, it falsely assumes that women not holding down 9-to-5 jobs cannot retire and therefore do not need retirement planning.

• One reason the myth may continue is that women sometimes lose their spouses early. The transition of widowhood is so traumatic that it hides the equally important second change that must be made.

• There is an impression that retirement should be the dessert that follows the full-course meal of earlier life. Maybe this is why pre-retirees view the transition as a piece of cake! Instead of thinking ahead to retirement, they make comments such as: "My retirement plan consists of putting all of my work problems in my briefcase and presenting them to my boss as a farewell present," or "Retirement is a pot of gold at the end of the rainbow. You don't have to plan for something that beautiful."

Many pre-retirees are so occupied with getting out of their career traps that they fail to understand what happens when they leave their jobs. Despite having planned other phases of their lives, they seem to feel that their retirement will take care of itself. The opposite is often true. For example, many retirees go back to work because they cannot handle leisure time. Learning to live without employment obligations and with a lot of free time on hand after retirement does not necessarily come easy.

For many years it has been suggested that some men put off retirement planning and retirement because they fear their wives will control their free time and their home. They anticipate, "Honey, do the dishes", "Honey, do the windows," and "Honey, take the dog to the vet." Normally, these individuals need not worry because most women don't want someone under foot, monitoring their activities and invading their space. One wife expressed it well: "The only time you will ever hear me use that "Honey, do" expression is when I say, "Honey, do something on your own, away from the house, so we can both have room to breathe." Spouses need the same autonomy after retirement that they did before.

Some conscientious individuals who have worked hard all their lives feel that they are home-free when they retire. They say: "I've done my bit for society; now it's society's turn," or "I paid my dues through church work for 30 years, now the church can take care of me." They operate under the premise that you pay your dues during your working years and then draw interest. A nice dream but, sadly, life doesn't work that way. In fact, happy retirees often pay more dues, not less. They contribute more to charitable organizations and communities than they did when they were working. The most successful retirees are those who have an opportunity to repay society by sharing their talents.

Some retirees who discover that their finances are insufficient for the luxury of a lifestyle without an active income become attracted to real estate as a new profession like children in a candy store. You repeatedly hear: "I'm working on my real estate license to supplement my retirement income by working a few hours a week. All I need to do is sell a few homes each year. Best of all, it won't interfere with my leisure activities."

This amuses professional realtors who understand that these new faces will not offer real competition. Selling real estate is not a part-time career; it is difficult and time consuming, and it should not be considered an aspect of your retirement plans. The professionals say either be in the field seriously or get out. Many retirees attempt real estate careers for a while and then painfully lower their sights or give up.

Few invest the time required to become successful.

Years ago, inflation should have exploded the myth that there are no financial worries after retirement. But people did not get the message that retirement economics are tough. It is not uncommon to hear statements such as "My taxes will be lower," and "Senior discounts are everywhere." Such ideas are not a retirement plan. Nor is, "Think of the money I'll save doing repairs myself, now that I'm not working and I have time," or "We'll buy less meat and improve our health."

Although there are some financial advantages after retirement, certain factors continue to be ignored. What about the problem of having more time to spend less money? What about increased expenses for home, car, and medical insurance? Utility bills? Medical care not covered by insurance?

Unfortunately people don't have trial retirements to test how far their money will go. If they did, they would discover that retirement dollars do not stretch any further than pre-retirement ones, and there are usually fewer of them.

8

Eight Steps to Saving for Retirement

There are many things that you could do to save for retirement, and I have outlined eight key steps that I believe can be most effective. Without a doubt, the earlier you start the better off you will be. That's because planning early generally means that you will amass more funds that will later be available to support your retirement lifestyle.

1. Start planning for retirement early

Think about how you want to live and where.

Calculate how much money you think you will need to do that. Take into consideration how many years you anticipate until retirement, and remember that the cost of living will go up during the time.

Put time on your side; the sooner you start saving, the more time your money has to grow. Make retirement savings a high priority by setting goals for yourself, devising a plan, and sticking to it. Remember, it's never too early or too late to start saving. So start now, whatever your age!

2. Plan for the possibility of living longer

Don't overlook the possibility of living on a fixed income for as long as 20 or 30 years. We'd all like to think that we'll live forever. Interesting enough, when many people plan their retirement, they cost it out based on leaving this world by a certain age. Usually they look at family history and personal health. But if someone calculates the costs to live until the age of 84, money is going to run out if he lives through his 95th birthday. So if you start off by planning to live a long life, you can enjoy those years much more because you planned for it, and you prepared yourself financially.

3. **Create a financial plan**

It is generally recommended to work out the finances either together with a certified financial planner or with computer software programs designed for this purpose. Proper planning will help you figure out how much money you should set aside or invest on a regular basis for retirement. Don't forget all expected post-retirement financial support, including government benefits.

4. **Contribute funds weekly, monthly or annually to your employer's 401(k) plan or your SEP-IRA**

Be sure to consider a Roth IRA or a traditional IRA (as explained elsewhere in this book) if you qualify. If your employer offers a tax-sheltered savings plan, such as a 401(k), sign up and contribute as much as you can. Your taxes will be lower, your company may kick in more, and automatic deductions make it easier. Over time, compound interest and tax deferrals make a big difference in the amount you will accumulate.

If your employer doesn't offer a retirement plan, suggest that it start one. Simplified plans can be set up by certain employers. For information on simplified employment pensions, order Internal Revenue

Service Publication 590 by calling 1.800.829.3676, or view a copy on the IRS website.

5. Pay off major debts

As quickly as possible, pay off debts such as home mortgages, college loans, and other significant cash-flow drains. The sooner you take care of these, the less interest you will pay, and the more you will have for retirement.

6. Cut back

As you approach retirement, you may want to reduce your discretionary expenses and try to live on a fixed income. Adjust your asset allocation based on your spending patterns. If you are spending more than your assets are earning, you may have to lower spending or take more risks in the hope of increasing your returns.

7. Don't touch your savings

Don't dip into your retirement savings. If you do, you'll lose principal and interest, and possibly tax benefits. If you change jobs, roll over your savings directly into an IRA or your new employer's retirement plan.

8. **Save smart**

How you save can be just as important as how much you save. Inflation and the type of investments you make play important roles in how much you'll have to live on after retirement. Know how your pension or savings plan is invested, as knowledge and financial security go hand in hand.

These tips should point you in the right direction, but you'll still need more information. Talk to your employer, your bank, your union, or a financial advisor. Ask questions and make sure the answers make sense to you. Get practical advice and act now. Financial security doesn't just happen. It takes planning and commitment and, yes, money.

9

Reduce Your Credit
Card Debt

If you are like most Americans, chances are you have embedded yourself in credit card debt, and here are several fool-proof steps to reducing it.

1. Refrain or limit yourself from credit card use. This is just as hard as it sounds. The best tactic is to leave the credit cards at home when you go shopping, or make them very inconvenient to use. As an extreme, you can put them into a safety deposit box. Some peo-

ple even freeze their credit cards in blocks of ice!

2. Review all of your ongoing spending. When choked with credit card debt, it's important to differentiate between what's needed and what's not. What activities can you cut out? Create a budget and determine what expenses can be eliminated. Every little bit of saving helps and, over time, can add up to a real difference in what you owe.

3. Another tactic is to tackle the highest-rate loans and work your way down. This will reduce your debt load the fastest. However, this strategy, while making the most sense financially, is often hard to do. Experts say an alternative method involved initially working off one small balance, then moving on to the next one, and then continuing down the line.

4. Another helpful tactic that experts suggest is to negotiate lower rates. Get on the phone with your credit card issuer and see if you can convince them to lower your interest rate. True, this strategy won't work well if you have been late with your payments 10 times over the last year. But if you have been good with your payment schedule, you can tell them that you have a

rate that you're not happy with and that you're seeing better card rates in the mail every day. If they hesitate, don't waste your time trying to convince someone without authority. Ask to speak to the manager, then plead the case again. Remind them that you have been a good customer, have a good credit score, and that you are seeing offers from competitors all the time. It doesn't always work but it often can. After all, it's in their interest to help you.

5. You can also think about a balance transfer. Look around for a low-rate card but remember to read the fine print. Does the low rate apply just to the balance transfer, or for new purchases also? Are there balance transfer fees? If so, how much? What are the annual fees? What happens if you're late on a payment? Consider a card that offers 12 months of interest-free payments or gives you a low, fixed interest rate over the life of the transferred balance. But always read the fine print!

6. Set up a new payment schedule. This is one of the best approaches, if your credit card company permits it: pay your debt bi-monthly, instead of once a month, to cut back the amount of interest you are paying. If

you can't afford to pay more than you're already paying each month, simply break your current payment amount into two payments and make the payments twice a month, instead of once. For example, if you now pay $60 a month towards you credit card, start paying $30 at the beginning of the month and $30 in the middle of the month, and you will actually save on interest.

7. Consider reducing the amount of money you are investing and/or saving in order to pay off debts. This is a good idea if you're paying more interest on your debt than what you're earning with your savings and/or investments. Once you've paid off your high interest debt, you can bump up the amount you are putting away and investing, and resume your savings plan.

10

Reduce Your Mortgage Debt

As the mortgage market continues to deteriorate in the current housing slump, many people are finding it difficult to make their mortgage payments. It is no secret that foreclosure rates have skyrocketed during the past year, especially among sub-prime mortgage holders or poor credit borrowers. This is a result of the many people who took on more expensive loans than they could afford, and others who dove into adjustable rate mortgages they did not understand. If your mortgage is putting a stranglehold on your bank account, or if you are looking to get an affordable mortgage, consider the suggestions offered in this chapter.

Reducing your mortgage burden involves changing your overall financial mindset. Americans have a "buy now, pay later" way of thinking. It is likely that you spend more than you earn. There seems to be a consensus that it is okay to put yourself in debt to enjoy all the pleasures of today. While there is really no escaping the hefty debt of a mortgage if you want to be a homeowner, waiting and saving for other purchases can make mortgage debt more manageable. Mortgage lenders often use the 28/36 ratio to determine how much debt you should be carrying. Only 28% of your monthly salary should go toward your housing costs, while your total debt obligations, including mortgage payments, should not exceed 36% of your monthly income.

Take a look at the things you are currently buying on credit. If it is a choice between keeping your house or "extras" like a new car or the big screen TV, which would you choose? Often delaying some of your wants will free up the cash you need to more easily afford your mortgage.

A large proportion of your monthly mortgage payment goes toward interest charges. While you cannot decrease the amount of principal required, you can reduce the amount of interest you have to pay. If you have the extra funds available each month, you could refinance into a shorter loan, such as a 15 or 20-year fixed rate loan. This would raise your monthly payments in the short term, but it would save you thousands of dollars in interest over the long term. If you don't have quite that much on hand, you could consider making an extra mortgage payment at least once a year. This will also help you cut out some of the interest charges and you won't have to pay closing costs for the refinance.

If you absolutely need access to more money and you have equity built up in your home, consider going with a home equity loan rather than a home equity line of credit (HELOC). Because of the stressed market conditions, home equity loans today carry rates lower than HELOCS, so you will pay less interest with an equity loan. And an equity loan gives you a lump sum with a predictable repayment schedule. A HELOC allows you to draw money as needed for a certain period of time, but it will probably tempt you to borrow more than you actually need.

When you refinance your mortgage, you take out a new home loan and use some or all of the proceeds to pay off the existing one. If you obtain a lower interest rate on your new loan than you had on the former, you'll be saving money.

Generally, there are two situations when it is wise to refinance your mortgage. Periods of rising interest is one such time, if you have an adjustable rate mortgage. If you refinance to a fixed rate mortgage, particularly to a rate similar to your present low adjustable rate, you'll avoid the higher costs when the adjustable rates start going up.

The other ideal time to refinance is when you'll save money by getting a lower interest rate. In that case, you'll want to make sure that your monthly savings will pay back your refinancing costs while you're still living on the property. If you sell your home before your refinancing has paid for itself, you won't be saving anything.

If you are experiencing cash flow difficulties, you may be tempted to lower your monthly mortgage payments by refinancing to extend the term of the loan. From a savings perspective, this is not a good reason to refinance. Unless you get a lower interest rate on the new loan as part of the bargain, you're not really saving any money; in fact, the reverse will be true. If you extend the terms of your mortgage without changing anything else, you might relieve your tight cash flow situation, but you'll actually pay more total interest on the mortgage in the long run.

Your refinancing cost is the total of any points, closing costs, and private mortgage insurance (PMI) premiums that you pay when you take out the new loan. In addition, any lost tax savings must also be regarded as part of the cost of refinancing.

There are times when lenders offer "no points, no closing costs" refinancing deals. Check the terms of these offers carefully to make sure that you understand what's involved.

Points are prepaid fees. One point equals 1% of the amount you're borrowing, and any points you're charged are usually deducted from the mortgage proceeds you receive. Mortgage lenders typically charge one point as a loan origination fee. Beyond that, lenders may charge additional points on loans with interest rates below the current market rate. By doing so, the lender makes a little more money up-front, and you get a lower interest rate on your mortgage. If you're going to stay in your house for a long time and can afford to do so, paying more points in the beginning may get you a better interest rate and save you more money in the long run.

Your closing costs include a variety of fees for services such as an appraisal, a title search, recording, and other costs associated with processing and finalizing your mortgage. If your loan-to-value ratio is greater than 80% of the appraised value of your property, you may also be required to carry PMI. The premiums for this insurance usually become a portion of your new monthly mortgage payment and thus reduce your savings from refinancing. In addition, you may discover hidden costs. For example, if you're paying less interest on your new mortgage, you'll have less to deduct on your income tax return. If this makes your tax payments higher, your savings will be offset further.

Once you've determined what your refinancing costs will be, you can then determine how long it will take for your refinancing to pay for itself. To do so, divide the total of the points and closing costs that you paid by the net monthly savings that the new loan provides you. Your net monthly savings will be your interest savings less any PMI premiums and tax advantage losses (expressed as monthly figures).

For example, assume you refinanced $200,000. You paid two points and total closing costs of $1,800. You got a great interest rate on the loan, so you'll save

$80 a month in interest charges. However, your PMI premiums are now $10 per month higher, and you've lost tax savings of $120 a year, or $10 per month. Your refinancing costs are $3,800 - two points of $1,000 each and $1,800 in closing costs. Meanwhile, your net savings are $60 per month - $80 per month saved interest less $10 per month increased PMI premiums and $10 per month lost tax savings. If you divide $3,800 by $60, you'll find your refinancing will pay for itself in a little over 63 months.

No-cash-out refinancing occurs when the amount of your new loan doesn't exceed your current mortgage debt (plus points and closing costs). With this type of refinancing, you can typically borrow up to 95% of your home's appraised value.

A cash-out refinancing occurs when you borrow more than what you owe on your existing mortgage. In this case, you are often limited to borrowing no more than 75-80% of the appraised value of your property. Any excess proceeds remaining after you've paid off an existing mortgage can be used in any way you choose, but the best use might be to pay off other outstanding high-interest debt, such as credit card debt.

Cash-out refinancing has certain advantages.

The interest rate that you'll pay on the mortgage proceeds will usually be less than the interest rate on the other debts (i.e. car loans, personal loans, credit cards, and even some student loans). Moreover, the interest paid on your refinanced mortgage is generally tax deductible, whereas the interest on consumer debt is not.

There are disadvantages to this approach, too. Your refinanced mortgage is secured by a lien on your home. If you can't make the mortgage payments, the lender can foreclose on your home and sell it to pay the mortgage. Credit card or automobile lenders can't take your house away in this fashion. Moreover, unless you're well disciplined, you could pay off the high interest (credit card) debt only to run it up again, further damaging your financial position.

If you're going to explore a cash-out refinancing, do it only if all of the following are true:

• Your savings make the refinancing worthwhile, even if it wouldn't give you the chance to repay other debt.

• Your savings are "real", due to a lower interest rate or a shorter loan term, and not due solely to tax factors, since tax laws may change.

• You're confident that you can afford the new monthly mortgage payment.

• You trust yourself (and your spouse) not to run up the repaid debt again.

Even if the rate on a new mortgage would be only slightly lower that what you have now, refinancing is a good idea if your savings will outweigh the costs of refinancing during the time you own the home. If you're unsure how much longer you might live in a particular locale, use recouping your refinancing costs in five years or less as a good rule of thumb.

Another secret of reducing your mortgage payments is making early and consistent extra payments. For example, on the home mortgage example previously used, if you pay an additional $100 each month you will save over $82,000 in interest payments. Not only that, but you will also have your home paid off nine years and two months earlier. You knock nearly 10 years off your mortgage just by paying an extra $100 a month.

Well, that $100 extra you pay the first month would have cost you about $270 in interest to borrow for 30 years. Since you have paid it already, you can reduce your last mortgage payment by $270. The next month's extra payment will reduce your last mortgage payment by $268. Each month as you pay that extra $100, your final mortgage payment will be reduced until you won't need to make a final payment, then the second to last payment, then third to last and so forth. Soon you will have shaved years and thousands of dollars in interest charges off your mortgage.

That's great, but maybe you can't spare $100 each month. How about $50, $25, or even $10? An additional payment of $50 each month will save you five years and seven months and about $52,000 dollars. $25 each month will cut your time by three years and three months, saving you about $30,000. Just $10 a month will reduce your time by one year and three months, and save you over $13,500.

Every little bit helps. Some months you may only be able to add $10 to your payment; some months you may be able to add $200. And this applies to interest on credit card payments or any other kind of debt repayment. Paying down as much of the principal (or the amount you owe) each month will help reduce the interest you are charged and the length of time it takes to pay off the debt.

So why don't credit card companies charge you

more of the principal each month? If you were making 18% on an investment, wouldn't you want this investment to last as long as possible? Of course! So do the credit card companies. They are happy for you to pay off your balance, but even more excited for you to keep paying them that 18% interest.

Here are some other interesting tips and tricks:

• One trick your mortgage company might have played on you is to include a pre-payment penalty in your mortgage. If you try to pay off your mortgage early, they may actually charge you for doing so. Or they may only apply part of your payment to the principal and take the rest as a "service charge".

• Make sure that when you make an additional payment, you send a check separate from your monthly mortgage payment, with instructions that the amount is to be applied toward the principal of your loan. Otherwise they may just apply it towards next month's payment and still charge you the interest.

• Generally you will not have this problem with credit card companies. But watch out for late payments or going over your credit limit. They may then use these "rule infractions" as cause to raise your rate to over 25%!

• If you are looking to refinance your mortgage, look for a mortgage that lets you pay on a bi-weekly basis. Since many people receive a bi-weekly paycheck, this also makes it easier to budget your money. If you are paying every two weeks you will make an additional monthly payment each year (26 bi-weekly payments vs. 12 monthly payments). Also, because you are paying the principal down every two weeks rather than every month, your interest charges will be reduced.

You CAN take control of your interest charges. Make those extra monthly payments. The feeling of being debt-free will far outweigh the temporary pleasure of that extra burger, movie or new DVD-player!

Mortgage Checklist: Things To Think About

1. Can you afford to have a mortgage?

2. Is this the right type of mortgage for you?

3. What impact does it have on your cash flow and other goals?

4. Does it suit your financial plan/strategy?

5. Should you use principal and interest or an interest-only loan?

6. Are fixed loans or variable loans more suitable?

7. How can you pay this loan off faster?

8. Can you get a better rate by refinancing?

9. What would be the benefit of refinancing, and what is the best way to do it?

11

Reduce What You Spend on Health Insurance

By taking some important first steps, such as losing weight, quitting smoking, eating in a more healthy manner, wearing seat belts, and exercising, you may be able to eliminate the necessity for several health insurance components. After you have done all that you could to keep yourself in good physical shape, below are some suggestions for reducing your health insurance costs.

1. Choose the right health insurance plan.

Don't make the mistake of focusing only on keeping monthly premiums down. Try to factor in realistic deductibles and co-payments. Here is a snapshot of some of the employee health insurance plans:

HMO. A health maintenance organization is best if you and your family generally don't have complex medical issues, mostly use general practitioners, are satisfied with the selection of doctors in the plan's network (because going outside the network might mean loss of coverage), and/or need a lot of routine care, such as check-ups for young children.

PPO. A preferred provider organization is best if you have a medical problem that requires specialists, and/or your favorite doctors are out of the network. PPOs cover non-network doctors, although co-payments and deductibles are higher than with HMOs.

POS. A point-of-service plan, which combines features of HMOs and PPOs, is best if you and your family are healthy and need routine care, but want the flexibility of going out of the network. With a POS, you can see any doctor you want. Your share of the cost is usually a percentage of the total bill.

FSA or HSA. If you want to save on health insurance, you should consider a Flexible Spending

Account. You can put away tax-free dollars to cater to your health needs. Any unused amount could be carried over into the next year, still tax free. This enables you to build a large reserves of funds for your health needs, without having to give the government a piece of your pie. Some companies offer HSAs, which combine a high-deductible ($1,050/year or more) low-premium health insurance plan for large hospital bills, with a tax-free savings account for smaller medical costs, such as doctor visits.

HSA holders could contribute up to $2,700 a year ($5,450 for families) as recently as 2006, and those between 55 and 65 years old were allowed to put in an additional $700. Unused money can be carried over from year to year and invested where it can grow without being taxed.

An HSA is especially good for older workers who want to accumulate money for post-retirement health-care costs or for long-term-care insurance premiums. The self-employed can write off health insurance premiums and HSA contributions as business expenses. More benefits are explained in IRS publication number 969, Health Savings Accounts and Other Tax-Favored Health Plans (800-TAX-FORM, www. irs.gov/publications).

While we want to lower our healthcare costs, we also need to ensure that we safeguard our health and our lives. If you're reasonably healthy, don't visit the doctor very often and don't need to use expensive medications, consider switching to a higher deductible to save on premium costs. By increasing your deductible from $100 to $200, you can cut your premium payment down significantly.

If you opt to pay your premiums monthly, you will pay higher rates. Although this alternative is always more convenient, it costs more. There are transaction charges that are incurred when processing a check, so while a yearly payment attracts just one check and therefore one transaction per year, monthly payments attract twelve. This implies that you'll pay transaction charges 12 times instead of once. There are also administrative costs to your insurer that result just from taking monthly payments. A good example is the expenses associated with mailing payment notices. Such costs are incorporated into your rate, thereby making it higher than if you paid every year.

2. Review hospital bills.

If you have to be hospitalized, before going home request an itemized bill. Ask for explanations of vague terms such as "lab fees" or "miscellaneous fees". Compare the bill to your log and the explanation of benefits (EOB) from your insurance company. If the hospital billing department doesn't correct discrepancies, speak to the Patient Ombudsman.

3. Hire a professional medical claims advocate if your medical bill is very high and complex.

You can find one in your area by contacting Medical Billing Advocates of America (304-645-6389/www.billadvocates.com) or Alliance of Claims Assistance Professionals (www.claims.org). The typical cost for an advocate is $30 or more an hour.

4. Lower Medication Costs.

You can lower your medication costs if you buy your prescriptions on-line, and cheaper prices are also offered for purchases made by phone. Companies that work through the Internet have lower overhead than brick-and-mortar businesses, so they can sell at reduced prices. Verify to ensure you are buying from a good company, using a resource like the Better Business Bureau.

The use of unapproved medications will increase your healthcare costs, and misusing them also will make you spend more on health insurance. In addition, stay away from self-medication, which will make you pay much higher rates.

5. Group insurance plans are more affordable.

Individuals who have the opportunity to use a group plan can receive lower rates than if purchasing just for themselves. The higher your risk, the more you'll save if you use a group plan.

A group plan will save you a significant amount if you have a health condition that makes individual health insurance either too expensive or almost impossible to get. A group plan is a good way to lower your premium without bringing down the quality of coverage you get.

6. Spouse's Employment Coverage.

As a general rule, if your spouse has health coverage from his or her employer, it probably provides better and less expensive coverage than you could get on your own.

7. Shop on-line.

By offering insurance products on-line, insurance companies save on broker and agent fees. Often, this translates into premium savings for policies purchased over the Internet. So when your fingers do the walking, make sure they do so on a keyboard and not in the Yellow Pages!

8. Medical Savings Accounts (MSA).

Under the Health Insurance Portability and Accountability Act (HIPAA), if you're self-employed you may be eligible for a medical savings accounts. MSAs work in conjunction with higher deductible health insurance policies to reduce premiums and allow you to use pre-tax dollars to pay for medical expenses up to the limit of the deductible on your insurance policy.

Basically, you reduce your premium by replacing a low-deductible policy with one that has a high-deductible, and use the premium saving to make fully tax-deductible contributions to your MSA. Individuals can contribute up to 65% of the deductible each year into an MSA (75% for families). The money goes into a tax-deferred account or trust and you pay your medical expenses (until you reach the deductible) by drawing from the account. Of course, once you hit the deductible, the insurance policy kicks in.

If you spend less than what you contributed,

the surplus stays in the account and earns interest. Moreover, the funds can be invested in high-return vehicles such as mutual funds and stocks.

As the balance can be carried forward, an MSA can be used to accumulate a pretty healthy nest-egg for retirement. In fact, a *Journal of Financial Planning* analysis calculated that if you contribute $1,500 per year into an MSA for 25 years, based on a 12% rate of return, you'll end up with almost $1.5 million. That's assuming you don't draw from it to pay for medical costs, of course.

MSAs offer a very tax-effective and potentially lucrative way to self-fund part of your healthcare costs while dramatically reducing your premiums. If luck is on your side and you remain healthy, by the time you reach retirement age, your MSA could well fund your retirement.

12

How to Cut Your Car Insurance Costs

Paying less insurance each year can cost you more in the long term. For your protection, buy car insurance coverage that will pay at least $100,000 per person and $300,000 per accident. If you have sizable assets, consider increasing those limits to $250,000 per person and $500,000 per accident. Such added coverage will raise your premium at least 10%. It is recommended that people with a high net worth have a separate "umbrella" policy to insure against a lawsuit that is pursuing an amount beyond their car policy's limits. You may need to buy higher insurance limits to qualify for an umbrella policy.

Property damage.

This coverage pays to repair or replace another person's vehicle or other property damaged by your car. Most states typically require only $10,000 to $25,000, but my research leads me to suggest buying coverage of $100,000.

Uninsured and under-insured motorist coverage.

This covers medical bills, rehabilitation, and funeral costs, as well as losses for pain and suffering for you or the passengers in your car when an accident is caused by a hit-and-run driver or someone who has little or no insurance. Buy the same amount of this coverage as you do bodily injury coverage. That way, if someone who has no insurance hits you, your medical costs will be covered.

The following are the insurance policies you'll probably need:

• **Collision and comprehensive.**

Collision coverage pays to repair or replace your car, no

matter who or what caused the accident. Comprehensive insurance pays to repair or replace your car if it's damaged as a result of a storm or other natural event, or if it is stolen. Coverage kicks in for the amount above your deductible. Your best option is to choose the highest deductible you can afford to pay out of pocket - at least $500. Once the cost of this coverage equals 10% of your vehicle's book value, you might want to cancel it, since you will collect no more than your vehicle's market worth. Antique vehicles or cars with collector value sometimes are insured through a separate rider, or you may have to find a separate specialty insurer.

• Personal injury protection.
PIP reimburses you for lost wages and in-home care needed as a result of an accident. If you have separate health and disability policies, you can just buy the state-required minimum for PIP. The other policies should cover the balance of your needs.

• Medical payments coverage.
Sometimes called med-pay, this covers medical bills for you and your passengers, regardless of who's at fault. When this coverage isn't automatically included

in your policy, its costs are minimal. You may not require any if you have good health insurance. To protect passengers who may not have their own health coverage, you may want to carry at least $5,000 of this coverage.

• Roadside assistance.

This coverage pays to have your vehicle towed. If you already have an car-club membership or your car's manufacturer provides this service for free, don't buy this extra coverage.

• Rental reimbursement.

This coverage typically costs $30 per year and pays for a rental car - usually for up to 30 days - if your vehicle is stolen or is in the shop for repairs sustained in an accident. There's usually a cap on the amount you're reimbursed per day and per occurrence.

Money-saving tips:

• Ask for the top tier.

Insurers sort customers according to their likelihood of filing a claim, and then assign them to one of several categories commonly referred to as tiers. Top-tier customers, such as those who have had few or no claims in the past several years and live in neighborhoods where car-theft rates are low, can easily save 15% or more off the standard rate. But simply because you qualify initially or improve your driving record doesn't mean you automatically get top-tier status.

• Check the insurance rates before you buy a car.
The difference in premiums between one vehicle and another can be substantial. Much of that has to do with the cost of repairing collision damage, which can vary greatly even among seemingly similar vehicles.

• Get equipment discounts.
You may qualify for extra discounts if your car has safety equipment such as air bags or anti-lock brakes. Also, ask your insurance company or agent about anti-theft equipment such as an alarm system, which can usually get you a discount on the comprehensive part of your coverage.

• Group your policies with one insurer.
Most insurers will give you a multiple-policy price break if you let them write your car, home, and personal liability coverage.

• **Improve your driving skills**.

Completing a certified defensive-driving course can reduce your premium in some states.

• **Utilize academic performance.**

If you have children who drive, you can save on your insurance bill if they get good grades or if they attend a school located more than 100 miles from your home and don't use the car there.

• **Group discounts**.

Insurers award discounts to low-risk consumers who share a common affiliation such as a membership in an employee group, a company pension fund, or an alumni association. These so-called affinity discounts can be sizable, so if they apply to you, it pays to take advantage of them. Ask your insurer if you qualify for such a discount through any of the groups with which you are affiliated. Alternatively, ask representatives of the groups or associations to which you belong if they have arrangements with any insurance companies.

• **Keep repair options open.**

Some insurers insist that you use generic replacement parts or they encourage you to bring your vehicle to certain body shops in an effort to cut claims costs. While this arrangement may lower your premium, you may want to preserve your flexibility by insuring with a company that lets you decide which parts are used (original equipment or after-market copies), and who makes the repairs. In tests conducted a few years ago, investigators found that none of the after-market replacement bumpers tested fit as well as factory-original bumpers or stood up as well to low-speed impacts. They also had trouble making generic fenders fit properly.

As you can see, with research, information and persistence, you can reduce your car insurance costs.

13

Cut Your Life
Insurance Costs

Although term life insurance does not build cash-value or have the tax benefits like universal or whole life insurance options, it can be a great option for someone who wants life insurance but can't afford the higher premiums that other insurance programs may offer. Here is a check-list to help you decide if a low-cost term life insurance policy could be right for you:

• You're on a budget and cannot afford a very high premium.

• You're young and in good health.

• You're looking for a simple, straight-forward, low-cost life insurance plan to protect your beneficiaries.

When talking with your agent about term life insurance, ask a lot of questions. Generally, agents do not receive as much commission on term life insurance as they do on cash-value policies, so you may have to probe a little for more information.

Having a single-life insurance policy instead of several small ones will save you money. You may be juggling quite a few life policies at once - an employee group policy, an individual policy you've purchased, or a policy started for you as a child.

Although you might think it makes more financial sense to have several policies with small death benefits and lower premiums, if they are all under your name then consolidating them can save you money. Shop around for one policy with a death benefit worth the combined amount of all the current policies in your name.

A first-to-die policy covers both spouses. The

death benefit is paid to the surviving spouse when either one dies. If the premiums are much lower than if you buy two individual policies, this could be a viable alternative as a money-saving device.

When it comes to insurance, there is little you can alter in terms of the death benefit. You should never decrease the amount of coverage if it means jeopardizing your family's security. However, there is one trick to access low-cost life insurance.

If your death benefit is near a multiple of $250,000, round up to the nearest $250,000. You should probably fiddle around with the coverage amount, checking out how each plan varies when you increase your death benefit by increments of $1,000. Often, once you reach a certain amount, the premium rate drops significantly. It is worthwhile to call the insurance company and request this information.

No matter how tempting it may be, do not provide any false information on your life insurance application in order to obtain a lower rate. If the insurance company discovers any distortion of the truth, your policy can be canceled and your premiums will not be reimbursed. Insurance companies can use cause of death (if it is smoking-related yet you claimed to be a non-smoker) as grounds for not honoring a policy.

And if you claim not to drink much, they can also use citations for DUIs or DWIs as justification for increasing premiums or denying continued coverage. If your health is adversely affected by smoking or drinking, perhaps you should quit now and reap the twenty to thirty percent savings!

14

Reduce What You Spend on Home Insurance

Home insurance is an important part of home-ownership. You don't need to pay top dollar for it, though. If you follow these tips, you can save a considerable amount of money:

1. Shop around.
It'll take some time, but could save you a good sum of money. Ask your friends, check the Yellow Pages, or contact your state insurance department to get a list

of companies to review. The National Association of Insurance Commissioners has a tremendous amount of valuable information, including complaints against insurance companies, to help you choose an insurer in your state. Many states also provide the frequency of consumer complaints by company.

It is important to check the financial stability of the companies you are considering, which can be done through rating companies such as A.M. Best and Standard & Poor, or consult consumer magazines. When you've narrowed the field to three insurers, then begin to gather price quotes.

States often make information available on typical rates charged by major insurers, and you can also compare rates with consumer guides, insurance agents, insurance companies and on-line insurance quote services. This will give you an idea of price ranges and tell you which companies have the lowest prices.

Don't consider price alone. The insurer you select should not only offer a fair price, but also deliver the quality service you would expect if you needed assistance in filing a claim. In assessing service quality, use the complaint information and talk to a number of insurers to get a feeling for the service they give. Asking each one how they could lower your costs.

2. Raise your deductible.

A deductible is the amount of money you have to pay toward a loss before your insurance company starts to pay a claim, in accordance with the terms of your policy. The higher your deductible, the more money you can save on your premiums. Most insurance companies today recommend a deductible of at least $500. If you can afford to raise your deductible to $1,000, you may save as much as 25%. If you live in a disaster-prone area, your insurance policy may have a separate deductible for certain kinds of damage. For example, if you live on the East Coast, you may have a separate windstorm deductible; if you live in a state vulnerable to hurricanes, you may have a separate deductible for hurricanes; and if you live in an earthquake-prone area, your earthquake policy has a deductible.

3. Don't confuse what you paid for your house with rebuilding costs.

The land under your house isn't at risk from theft, windstorm, fire and the other perils covered in your home-owners policy. So don't include the land value in deciding how much homeowner's insurance to buy. If you do, you will pay a higher premium than you should.

4. Buy your home and car policies from the same insurer.

Some companies that sell homeowners, car and liability coverage will take 5 to 15% off your premium if you buy two or more policies from them. But make certain this combined price is actually lower than buying the different policies from different companies.

5. Make your home more disaster-resistant.

Find out from your insurance agent or company representative how you can lower your insurance by taking steps to make your home more resistant to natural disasters, according to your geographical location. For example, if you live on the East Coast where windstorms often damage homes, you may be able to save on your premiums by adding storm shutters, reinforcing your roof, or buying stronger roofing materials. Older homes can be retrofitted to increase their ability to withstand earthquakes. In addition, consider modernizing your heating, plumbing and electrical systems to reduce the risk of fire and water damage.

6. Improve your home security.

You can usually get discounts of at least 5% if you have a smoke detector, burglar alarm or dead-bolt locks. Some companies offer to cut your premium by as much as 15 or 20% if you install a sophisticated sprinkler system and a fire and burglar alarm that rings directly at the police, fire or other monitoring stations. These systems aren't cheap and not every system qualifies for a discount. So before you buy such a system, find out what kind your insurer recommends, how much the device would cost, and how much you'd really save on premiums.

7. Seek out other discounts.

Companies offer several types of discounts, but they don't all give the same discount in every states. For example, since retired people stay at home more than working people, they are less likely to be burglarized and may also spot fires in the home sooner. And retired people usually also have more time for maintaining their homes. So if you're at least 55 years old and retired, you may qualify for a discount of up to 10% from some companies.

8. Maintain a good credit record.

Establishing a solid credit history can cut your insurance costs. Insurers are increasingly using credit information to price homeowners' insurance policies.

In most states, your insurer must advise you of any adverse action, such as a higher rate, at which time you should verify the accuracy of the information on which the insurer relied. To protect your credit standing and potentially lower your insurance rates, pay your bills on time, don't obtain more credit than you need, and keep your credit balances as low as possible. Check your credit record on a regular basis, and have any errors corrected promptly so that your record remains accurate.

9. Stay with the same insurer.

If you've kept your coverage with a company for several years, you may receive a special discount for being a long-term policyholder. Some insurers will reduce their premiums by 5% if you stay with them for three to five years, and by 10% if you remain a policyholder for six years or more. But make certain to periodically compare this price with that of other policies.

10. Review the limits in your policy and the value of your possessions at least once a year.

You want your policy to cover any major purchases or additions to your home. But you don't want to spend money for coverage you don't need. If your five-year-old fur coat is no longer worth the $5,000 you paid for it, you'll want to reduce or cancel your floater (extra insurance for items whose full value is not covered by standard homeowners policies such as expensive jewelry, high-end computers and valuable art work) and pocket the difference.

11. If you are in a government insurance plan, look for private insurance.

If you live in a high-risk area (such as one that is especially vulnerable to coastal storms, fires, or crime) and have been buying your homeowner's insurance through a government plan, you should check with an insurance agent or company representative. You can also contact your state's Department of Insurance for the names of companies that might be interested in your business. You may find that there are steps you can take that would allow you to buy insurance at a lower price in the private market.

12. When you're buying a home, consider the cost of homeowner's insurance.

You may pay less for insurance if you buy a house close to a fire hydrant or in a community that has a professional rather than a volunteer fire department.

It may also be cheaper if your home's electrical, heating and plumbing systems are less than 10 years old. If you are buying a home on the East Coast, you may get a reduction on insurance if you purchase a brick home, because it's more wind resistant. If you live in an earthquake-prone area, look for a wooden frame house because it is more likely to withstand that type of disaster.

Choosing wisely could cut your premiums by 5 to 15%. Check the CLUE (Comprehensive Loss Underwriting Exchange) report of the home you are thinking of buying. These reports contain the insurance claim history of the property and can help you judge some of the problems the house may have.

Remember that flood insurance and earthquake damage are not covered by a standard homeowner's policy. If you buy a house in a flood-prone area, you'll have to pay for a flood insurance policy, which can cost an average of $400 a year. The Federal Emergency Management Agency (FEMA) provides useful information on flood insurance (www.FloodSmart. gov). A separate earthquake policy is available from most insurance companies, as the cost of the coverage will depend on the likelihood of earthquakes in your area. In California, the California Earthquake Authority provides this coverage and can give you more information.

If you have questions about insuring any of your possessions, be sure to ask your agent or company representative when you're shopping around for a policy. For example, if you run a business out of your home, be sure to discuss coverage for that business. Most homeowner's policies cover business equipment in the home, but only up to $2,500, and they offer no business liability insurance. Although you want to lower your homeowner's insurance cost, you also want to make certain you have all the coverage you need.

15

Reduce What You
Spend on Gasoline

While everyone complains about the cost of gasoline, many people aren't aware of some basic tips that can help reduce what you spend.

1. Avoid prolonged warming up of your car engine, even on cold mornings. 30 to 45 seconds is plenty of time.

2. Be sure the automatic choke is disengaged after the

engine warms up. Chokes often get stuck, resulting in a bad gas and air mixture.

3. Don't start and stop the engine needlessly. Idling your engine for one minute consumes the gas amount equivalent to when you start the engine.

4. Avoid "revving" the engine, especially just before you turn the car off. This wastes fuel needlessly and washes oil down from the inside cylinder walls, owing to the loss of oil pressure.

5. Eliminate "jack-rabbit" starts. Accelerate slowly when starting from a complete stop. To allow the carburetor to function at peak efficiency, don't push the pedal down more than 1/4 of the total foot travel.

6. Buy gasoline during the coolest time of day - early morning or late evening - when gasoline is densest. Keep in mind that gas pumps measure volumes of gasoline, not densities of fuel concentration, and you are charged according to volume.

7. Choose the type and brand of gasoline carefully. Certain brands provide you with greater economy be-

cause of better quality. Use the brands which seem most beneficial, even though they may not always appear to be the cheapest.

8. Avoid over-filling the gas tank, which can result in sloshing over and out of the tank, thereby wasting your money. If the fuel nozzle is automatic, never fill the gas tank past the first "click".

9. Drive economically: Exceeding 40 mph forces your car to overcome tremendous wind resistance, which wastes gas. Also, never exceed the legal speed limit. Primarily these limits are set for your traveling safety, but lower speeds are more gas efficient too. Traveling at 55 mph gives you up to 21% better mileage when compared to former legal speed limits of 65 mph and 70 mph. Traveling at fast rates in low gear can consume up to 45% more fuel than is needed.

Traffic lights are usually timed for your motoring advantage, so by traveling steadily at the legal speed limit you boost your chances of having the "green light" all the way.

Manual shift cars allow you to change to highest gear as soon as possible, letting you save gas if you "nurse it along". However, if you cause the engine to "bog down", premature wearing of engine parts occurs.

It is also worthwhile to keep windows closed when traveling at highway speeds. Open windows can cause air drag, reducing your fuel mileage by 10%.

Drive steadily, as slowing down suddenly or speeding up too quickly wastes fuel. This means you must avoid tailgating - the driver in front of you is unpredictable. Not only is it unsafe, but if affects your wallet if he slows down unexpectedly, forcing you to brake quickly and waste more gas. Think ahead when approaching hills. If you want to accelerate, do so before you reach the hill and not once you've started to climb.

10. Avoid rough roads whenever possible, because dirt or gravel rob you of up to 30% of your gas mileage. When there are alternate roads that are straight, use them. Comparing traveling distance differences, remember that corners, curves and lane jumping require extra gas. The shortest distance between two points is always a straight line.

11. Automatic transmissions should be allowed to cool down when your car is idling at a standstill, such as railroad crossings or long traffic

lights. Placing your gear into neutral position reduces the transmission strain and allows it to cool.

12. Park the car in a manner that, when you are ready to travel again, will allow you to start in forward gear; avoid reversing gear maneuvers to save gas.

13. Regular tune-ups can save you money, so check the owner's manual for recommended maintenance intervals. Special attention should be given to maintaining clean air filters, as diminished air flow increases gas waste. Also, periodically inspect suspension and chassis parts for occasional misalignment. In addition to being unsafe at high speeds, bent wheels, axles, bad shocks, and broken springs create engine drag and utilize more gas.

14. Pay attention to your tires. Remove snow tires during good weather seasons; traveling on deep tire tread will use more fuel. Throughout the year, keep your tires inflated to the maximum limit, and periodically each one should be spun, balanced and checked for out-of-round. When shopping for new tires, get large diameter tires for rear wheels. Radial designs are recognized fuel-savers; check the manufacturer's spec-

ifications for recommended maximum tire pressures.

15. Pay attention to the roof of your car. Rough surfaces disturb otherwise smooth air flow around a car's body. Remove vinyl tops, as they cause air drag. When buying a new car, keep in mind that a fancy sun roof also can disturb smooth air flow (and mileage).

16. Your car's air conditioning can reduce fuel economy by 10% to 20%. Heater fans, power windows and added seats increase the engine load, which then gives you less miles per gallon.

17. When not in use, remove excess weight from the trunk or the inside of your car including extra tires, back seats, and unnecessary heavy parts. Extra weight reduces mileage, especially when driving up inclines.

18. Car pools may make your traveling more enjoyable but, more important, they reduce the gas expense when riders help cover fuel costs. While travel companions offer conversation that helps to keep the driver alert, car pooling also reduces traffic congestion, thereby giving drivers easier maneuverability and greater "steady speed" economy. For best results,

distribute the passenger and baggage weight evenly throughout car.

19. During cold weather watch for icicles frozen to the car frame; up to 100 lbs. can be quickly accumulated! Snow and ice which are not removed from your car can cause tremendous wind resistance. Pouring warm water on the snow and ice can help melt it quickly.

20. Don't drive more than you have to. The simplest way to reduce unnecessary gas costs is to spend less time in your car. Keep a list of the errands you have to run and try to combine several short errands into one trip – if they are in the same neighborhood.

21. Final car tips that may help you cut the costs of gasoline:

> • Pay attention to what is going into your car.
>
> • Install pressure regulator valve (sold in car parts stores).
>
> • Use graphite motor oil.
>
> • Regardless of advertising claims, beware of oil additives. Instead, you should add Marvel Mystery Oil into gas fill-ups.
>
> • Investigate fuel/water injection methods and

products.

• Use special gas additives to prevent winter freezing of gas lines.

• Convert your V8 engine over to a V4. No special kits are needed!

16

Reduce What You Spend On Taxes

The first step to reducing your taxes is to determine whether you should itemize. Itemizing is an incredibly easy concept to understand, but the strategies behind it can be complicated. The rule for when to itemize is simple - it should be done if the total of your itemized deductions is greater than your standard deduction.

Your tax is based on your "taxable income". That's your total income after you've subtracted "above-the-line" deductions such as your Individual Retirement Account (IRA) or other qualified retirement-plan contributions, moving expenses, or alimony payments, as well as your personal exemption and either your standard deducation or your itemized deducations.

Your itemized deductions are sometimes referred to as "below-the-line" deductions. (Your adjusted gross income is "the line".) Clearly, the more you can deduct, the less you pay in taxes.

Some taxpayers must itemize, even if their deductions are less than the standard deduction. You must itemize your deductions if:

• You are married, filing separately, and your spouse itemizes.

• You are a U.S. citizen who can exclude income from U.S. possessions.

• You are a non-resident or dual-status alien.

• You file a short-period return because of a change in your accounting period.

There are five main categories of itemized expenses that you can deduct when filing tax returns:

1. Medical and dental expenses.

2. Taxes. These include state and local income taxes,

property taxes on real estate, intangible taxes (on the value of stocks and bonds you own), and personal property taxes on such things as cars. As of 2007, you were able to deduct either your state income taxes or your state sales taxes, but NOT both. (As of this writing, Congress has not yet decided whether to extend this break for 2008 and beyond.)

3. Interest expenses. For most people, these are limited to home mortgage interest payments, points (interest that's prepaid to buy a home), and some interest on investments and education expenses. For most taxpayers, the mortgage deduction is what lets them itemize. If you take out a 30-year, $140,000 mortgage at 6%, you will generate about $8,350 in deductible interest in the first year.

4. Charitable contributions. If you have donated money (or in-kind contributions) to a recognized non-profit, with tax deductible status from the IRS, make sure you have receipts to provide to your accountant or to submit with your tax returns.

5. Casualty and theft losses. The key, then, is to maximize the value of your itemized deductions. Here's where planning can put dollars in your pocket.

Some itemized deductions - including medical

expenses or miscellaneous deductions such as investment expenses, safe deposit fees, professional education, employee job-hunting expenses and tax-preparation fees - are not allowed until they exceed a certain "floor" amount.

The toughest "floor" to exceed is medical expenses. No medical expenses are allowed as itemized deductions except for the amount that exceeds 7.5% of your adjusted gross income. That means if you have an adjusted gross income of $100,000, the first $7,500 of your medical expenses doesn't count.

Sometimes, however, elective medical expenses can be accelerated or even deferred. Orthodontic payments for you or your dependents can often be extended, and they can always be accelerated. These expenses are deducted in the year they are paid, which may not necessarily be the year the service is rendered.

If you can already pass the 7.5% test for allowable medical expenses, or these expenses would put you over the minimum hurdle, then consider accelerating them. If you lack the cash, consider charging the expenses. On credit card charges, you are allowed the deduction in the year of the charge, not in the year that the charge is paid off. But don't automatically accelerate if it puts you over the 7.5% floor. Remember that allowable medical expenses are just one component of the package, and your total itemized deductions must exceed your standard deduction before you get any real additional benefit from them.

If you don't exceed the 7.5% floor or your total itemized deductions don't exceed your standard deduction this year, you should consider deferring your payments or any elective medical procedures. You get the use of the money, as well as any investment returns. Moreover, you may be able to use the deductions in the subsequent year when you revisit the itemization question.

Miscellaneous itemized expenses are also deductible only after they exceed a minimum "floor". In this case, it's 2% of your adjusted gross income. So, with an adjusted gross income of $100,000, your first $2,000 of miscellaneous itemized deductions won't count.

But here again, many of these deductions can be either accelerated or deferred. Miscellaneous itemized deductions can often be paid in the year of your choice.

Any voluntary expenditure can be accelerated or deferred. Your gifts to charity are the best example.

Whether your $1,000 pledge to your church or synagogue is sent on December 31 from last year or January 1 of this year makes little difference to the charity receiving the money. However, in the 25% bracket for 2007, it can make a $250 difference to your tax bill - but again, only if your total itemized deductions exceed your standard deduction. If I can qualify for itemizing my taxes, I want to accelerate my tax savings. A dollar not paid today is worth a lot more than a dollar not paid in the future.

Taking a loss on failing investments (stocks, real estate, even collectibles) may help you offset taxes you'll have to pay on other gains or income. You can use up to $3,000 of capital losses to offset ordinary income (your salary and interest income) every year. This applies to taxable accounts, not your IRA or 401(k).

Paper losses don't count, so you may want to sell some investments now. Also take into account stock dividends that you reinvested in the same company and brokers' commissions that may increase your loss.

When the stock market has had a bad year (in 2008 it was down about 40%, so some investors may have a lot more than $3,000 in losses), you can carry that loss forward to your next tax return - or indefinitely, if necessary. It's a gift that keeps on giving.

Now is the time to move your retirement funds into an account that lets you take the money out when you retire, without tax penalties. If you make less than $100,000 a year, you're eligible to convert all or a portion of your traditional IRA to a Roth IRA, which has tax benefits.

There's a slight catch: You'll have to pay a one-time conversion tax, but it will be a lot less this year since your account value has likely decreased significantly. Furthermore, you don't have to worry about paying an early withdrawal fee when making a conversion.

A key benefit of a Roth IRA is the tax-free savings. Contributions and earnings can be withdrawn without paying taxes after the age of 59 1/2 (for accounts that are at least 5 years old).

If you are out of work, now is the time to gather as many miscellaneous itemized deductions as you can and the many expenses related to the job search. (It's one of the rare things not prohibited by the Alternative Minimum Tax.) Consider all of the expenses related to the job hunt or professional development with the potential to be tax-deductible: subscriptions to professional journals, dues for professional organizations or unions, and tuition for job-related courses. If you haven't taken advantage of them, you can until December 31. But remember, miscellaneous itemized deductions must comprise at least two percent of your adjusted gross income to be deducted from your federal return.

Charities are facing difficult financial times, too, and it can be to your benefit. You can get some tax savings in return for your good will. Donating clothes, toys, household goods and other items to charity before the end of the year may help you when filing tax returns in April.

Need some help figuring out the fair market value of donated items? Go to the Salvation Army's website for a list of average prices at their stores. Software, such as Turbo Tax, can also help you determine the value of non-monetary donations in accordance with IRS guidelines.

If you're making a monetary contribution, the check needs to be postmarked by December 31. You can also put your donation on a debit or credit card by that date; just be sure to pay the credit card bill in full when it arrives.

Getting a huge refund in April is a welcome

windfall when it comes, but many taxpayers could use those extra dollars over the course of the year. Every year about 80% of taxpayers get a refund averaging over $2,300. That's a little bit of cushion you could use now. Use the withholdings calculator at the IRS website to make sure you aren't having too much money taken out of your paycheck, then inform your employer of any discrepancies.

It is important to always check with a tax advisor before making any big tax-related financial decisions. Ask friends and colleagues for referrals or look for a CPA/personal finance specialist. Now is the time to get some expert help with your year-end tax planning. There have been a number of tax law changes and there are likely to be many more under President Obama. You want to make sure that you temper your tax moves in these turbulent economic times and that they make sound financial sense for you.

When it comes to taxes, credits are the preferred way to cut your bill. While deductions, either itemized or standard, reduce your amount of taxable income, credits cut your actual tax bill, dollar-for-dollar. That's because credits come into play AFTER your tax liability is figured. So if you owe Uncle Sam $500, a $250 tax credit will cut your bill in half. Similarly, some credits are more valuable than others. Refundable credits may eliminate any tax you owe, and provide you with a refund. So even if your tax bill is zero, you could get money back from the Internal Revenue Service thanks to a refundable credit, including:

- •Earned income tax credit
- •Additional child tax credit
- •Credit for taxes withheld on wages

Non-refundable credits can take your tax down to nothing, but you can't get money back from the government. Popular non-refundable credits are:

- •Child tax credit
- •Child-care and dependent-care credit
- •Credit for the elderly or disabled
- •Retirement savings contributions credit
- •Adoption expenses credit
- •Hope and Lifetime Learning education credits

These credits can't be used to get a refund on your tax return. When your tax bill reaches zero, any leftover credit amount is wasted. With the adoption credit, however, you can carry forward unused amounts from year to year until the credit is absorbed or the carry-forward period expires, whichever is first.

The choice of your tax form also could affect your credit claims. Form 1040EZ filers can only claim the earned income credit. To get the benefit of the other credits, you must use Form 1040 or Form 1040A, and some of these credits require you to fill out additional forms.

If your 2008 income has declined, it may pay to revisit items that were previously limited for you. You might catch a break.

17

Create a Corporation to Save Money

If you work from home, have a small business, offer consulting services, or are legally considered self-employed in some other way, you can save money by creating a legal business entity for tax purposes. Your business could probably be making more money, but chances are you are paying higher taxes than you have to. Today, many people set up a corporation to protect themselves from lawsuits and liability. But more and more individuals are learning the benefits of setting up a corporation for its tax benefits, which is a legal and safe avenue for you to bring home more money.

As an individual, you pay higher tax rates than businesses, usually for the initial $75,000 of your income. If you set yourself up as a corporation, you can deduct expenses that are related to your business, such as travel/car costs, business entertaining, and office equipment. As a corporation, you can also create a tax-efficient pension fund for yourself, giving security for your retirement, and a corporate medical plan to cover your medical/dental insurance, which can save you significant money in taxes each year.

Where else can you save money? If you are currently paying money to help support your children or parents, you may be able to hire them as employees through a legal loophole and then deduct costs. Indeed, some of these expenses are currently deductible under your current tax status. But if you can create a corporation that serves as a 'holding place' for your income, then you increase the likelihood of paying lower taxes. The important thing is to be able to have an alternative to a high income for your personal tax returns.

Most people who decide to create a corporation choose to set up something called an "S corporation", which is preferred by many small businesses or self-employed people. Through an S corporation, the Internal Revenue Service allows you to take deductions on the early years of your business, when you may have had losses as you work to set yourself up.

Here is an example to help you understand this. You and your best friend Dave decide to open a business together, and you set it up as an S corporation. In the first year of working together, you have a high amount of expenses and you are just starting to build your company's reputation. Business is slow in getting off the ground, and you face a loss of $30,000. Because you have established an S corporation, you can split the loss on your personal tax returns, so that you demonstrate a $15,000 loss due to your business. The IRS will probably approve a deduction of several thousands dollars (but obviously not $15,000!), saving you money in both your state and your federal tax dollars.

This is one of the most significant benefits of setting up an S corporation. There are other small benefits that you can receive, in addition to all the deductions (medical, car, and so forth), to which you may be entitled.

To start reaping the benefits today, you have to set up your business as a Limited Liability Company

(LLC) or as a regular corporation (known as C corporation), and then apply to the IRS to be recognized as an S corporation. You can learn more from www. irs.gov, as well as downloading or requesting any relevant forms that you will need from the website. You should also verify that in your own state you don't have to make any separate applications to receive state approval for recognition as an S corporation.

18

Create Solid Income Through Supplemental Home - Based Work

You and your spouse both work nine to five on weekdays. Yet both of your paychecks are not enough to cover all your financial obligations and needs. You need to pay your rent, utilities, credit cards, car loans, mortgage, kid's school needs, groceries, and so on. There are just too many expenses to pay! Sounds familiar?

If you are finding it hard to make ends meet, you

may want to narrow the "gap" and supplement your income by running a business from home on weekends and in your spare time. A successful part-time supplemental business can help provide the needed additional cash flow for your household. Moreover, the experience will show if you have what it takes to become an entrepreneur. If you're lucky and the business takes off, you could even make it a full time venture and quit the 9 to 5 grind.

Here are some business ideas that you could do at home without much start-up cost:

1. Personal Fitness Trainer

Pilates, yoga, and tae-bo are a few of the popular activities in the ever-growing fitness craze. If you love working out and want to help others get fit, consider becoming a personal fitness trainer. A personal trainer helps clients set and achieve fitness goals, including workouts, diet and overall lifestyle. Trainers often price services by the length and number of sessions or by the goal, and prices can vary based on geographical location. The usual hourly rate is from $35 to $75 per hour, although established trainers catering to celebrities get as much as ten times that rate.

2. Cake Decorator

Beautifully decorated cakes are often the centerpiece of special occasions such as weddings, birthdays, anniversaries, holidays and other special events. It is the decorator's task to transform the ordinary cake into a focal point for such celebrations. You must have the skills and artistic flair to decorate cakes, as well as the tools and equipment to help you create and design the cake. Anyone who celebrates an occasion is your potential customer. To research your market, get in touch with wedding coordinators, bakeries and party organizers who may be able to include your cakes in their own services. Other potential customers include friends getting married, and individuals and businesses who arrange parties.

3. Freelance Writer

You can write articles for magazines, advertising copy for brochures, technical manuals and other literary products on weekends. Be creative in finding writing opportunities. For example, if you are a new bride-to-be, you can write articles for wedding and women's magazines about the process of preparing for a wedding. If your day job is computer programming, you can write articles about the programs that you are using.

Some writing projects will pay you by the hour - about $20 to $75 depending on your writing and marketing skills. Most, however, will pay you by the number of words (for articles, op-eds, short stories) or by a percentage of the selling price (for books). There are a number of available resources listing potential markets for various kinds of writing, including poetry, screenplays, articles, books, and websites. Start with the "Writer's Market" directory, which is published annually, to get a list of all publishers and literary agents, as well as their writing requirements.

4. Cooking Instructor

If you are an excellent cook and want to share your culinary love with others, consider giving cooking lessons. You can set-up shop in your own kitchen, or offer classes in another location, giving lessons on general cooking techniques or a specialized cuisine such as Italian, vegetarian, or desserts. You must be very knowledgeable about your cuisine specialization and creative in food presentations.

A cooking instructor's potential income ranges from $30 to $75 per hour. However, most instructors charge by the class, with the fee depending on the amount of time, the cost of the classroom and ingredients, and the size of the class.

5. Fundraiser

If you have excellent people skills and marketing talent, consider becoming a part-time fundraiser. You
can work for charities and non-profit organizations,
raising donations for them. The key to succeeding in
this business is being able to present yourself as trust-
worthy, making people feel that the money they give to
charities will indeed reach those charities. As a means
to regulate this industry, some states require a certifi-
cation or license before you can begin your fundrais-
ing work. You can be paid on an hourly rate of $20 to
$35, but most fundraisers are paid a percentage of the
funds they raise. The rates can be as low as 2% to as
high as 20% of the total amount raised.

6. Musician

If you can sing or play a musical instrument, you can
jump-start your musical career on weekends by playing solo or with a group. Your gigs can include parties,
nightclubs, bars, and even weddings. To get started,
monitor the classified ad section of your local newspaper for ads asking to book musicians or to replace
regular band members.

7. Tutoring Service

A tutor helps students understand their school lessons and gain additional knowledge about a subject. The main requirement is that you know more about the subject than your students. You can tutor children in school or even college students. To start in this business, you can volunteer to tutor others in your primary subjects. Once you've built your resources (such as books on the subject), ask for referrals from teachers and other students. You may also distribute brochures to parents informing them about your services. Tutorial services often earn $25 to $50 an hour, although you can also package services (such as a flat fee of $200 for on-call tutoring).

8. Tour Guide

If your area is a tourist spot, consider becoming a tour guide on weekends. It is better to focus on groups or individual travelers. Tour guides can earn between $25 and $70 per hour. As a tour guide, you will organize an itinerary that will help these travelers see and learn about your area. You can create camping tours, historic tours, nature adventure, or even a spy tour depending on the tourist attractions in your area. Once you've decided your area of tour specialization, it will be much easier to reach your target customers.

9. Personalized Children's Books

Parents and grandparents often want special gifts for their children. This business will fill that demand. You can create and market children's books that include the child's name and weave personal information into the story. Instead of creating the book and writing the story line yourself, you can buy illustrated books pages that you can personalize and sell. The main equipment that you will need includes a computer and printer.

10. Antique Restoration Service

Restoring antiques to their former glory is a lucrative business. You can find, restore and refinish furniture, automobiles, collectibles, and other products of the past. However, it requires a variety of skills and thorough knowledge of the antique pieces. Depending on your niche market, you may need to be highly skilled in woodworking, varnishing, painting, and other tools, techniques and knowledge. Starting part-time in this field can allow you to gain experience working on various pieces, while improving your skills.

Your potential customers will depend on the type of pieces that you restore, your experience and local opportunities. Most likely, you will work with private collectors, antique dealers, resellers, estates, galleries, and museums. Antique restorers typically charge between $35 to $75 an hour. Some restoration services are priced on the value added, particularly if an antique piece priced at $100 is restored into one worth $1,000.

11. Candle making

If you are interested in the creative craft of candle making, you can have a lucrative home business. According to the National Candle Association, candle retail sales in the United States alone are projected at over $2.3 billion, not including candle accessories. Candles have become a must-have accessory in every home for their practical and decorative elements, and are used by seven out of ten American households. They have become a popular give-away for birthdays, Christmas, and housewarmings. Once merely a hobby of candle enthusiasts, candles are now sold in gift and specialty stores, home furnishing stores, by mail order, craft shows and on the Internet.

While candles can be made at a relatively low cost, candle making is a time-consuming process and may require some space to work (your kitchen can both be dangerous and very messy). Some people purchase candles already made and add decorative touches such as pressed dried flowers to the outside. Research the kinds of candles that are being produced so you can develop your own unique candle line.

12. Antiques and collectibles dealer

If you are interested in antiques and period collectibles, this business is for you. Many people have earned income from scouring neighborhood flea markets and yard sales for valuable finds, and reselling them for a handsome profit. You need to be able to learn how to distinguish which items are a steal and which ones to pass up, as well as how to price the bargains that you find. Your start-up phase will be devoted to scouting for merchandise to re-sell. As your inventory grows, you can spend time marketing your finds. You can rent a small booth at the mall or flea market every weekend. The Internet has expanded the market for antiques and collectibles business, and you can open an on-line store or sell your finds on eBay.

13. Cut-flower business

Flowers are all around us, and work-at-home moms with botany skills are well-placed to profit from people's love for decorating their homes and tables with beautiful fresh flowers. Cut flowers are a huge business in many parts of the world, and you can profit from this business if you have a medium-sized garden with good soil. Begin by establishing your garden and plant perennials like chrysanthymums, carnations, orchids, evening primroses, or whatever flower type you fancy. You are ready to find customers once your garden is overflowing with mature blossoms.

14. Transcription services

A transcription service involves typing from recordings. There are basically five major markets for the home-based transcriptionist: academic, business, medical, legal and professional writers. Academic typing, which is the most readily available market and the most lucrative, normally covers everything from book reports, doctoral dissertations, grant proposals, course outlines and everything in between. Business and commercial typing includes menus for restaurants, consultants' reports, mailing lists, brochures, correspondence, and other documents. The field of medical transcription, which often requires completion of a course, demands knowledge of the terminology used, and includes filling out health insurance forms, transcribing medical reports, preparing case studies for doctors, typing pathology reports and helping medical/dental offices that are overloaded with work. If you have acquired legal experience, you may be marketable in a typing business specializing in legal documents. Transcription can be provided as part of a business service such as a secretarial/word processing service or office support service.

15. Handicrafts

If you are making crafts now for your enjoyment, think about kicking your hobby into a higher gear and turning it into a profit-generating endeavor. Experts in the handicraft field estimate that the crafts industry generates almost $10 billion in annual sales. Depending on your craft, you can sell your products retail, wholesale, or at one-of-a-kind stalls at fairs, bazaars, and boutiques, as well as via mail-order catalogs, gift shops and department stores.

The challenge for many craft enthusiasts is turning their hobbies into full-blown businesses, and developing a more professional attitude toward their home business. Finding the right price for their products is always a difficult task, but the cardinal rule is to always make at least twice as much as you have paid for your supplies. Keep up-to-date with the latest trends by reading crafting magazines and try to find your own "niche" market for your crafts.

16. Niche newsletters

Small newsletters are emerging to serve the many needs of different groups - from silk painting to parenting twins to stock options. If you have special talents (like writing), live in a specific location (such as a key tourist area), or have specialist knowledge in a particular area (for example, money saving tips), you can publish your very own newsletter and earn money from it. Your newsletter need not be extravagantly designed or extremely colorful, but it must be well designed and readable.

Your first step is to find a valuable topic that will sell. By far, saving money and making money are two of the best topics for newsletters. There must be something in your idea that will compel audiences to buy your publication. Will it help them improve their lives and can they learn anything from it? It is also important if yours is a researchable topic to ensure longevity of your home business. Your idea must have a large potential audience, and there must be a way to reach your target market.

17. Home sewing

Consumer interest in sewing and crafting continues to expand. According to the Home Sewing Association, this is fueled by the current interest in home-based activities, the technical appeal of sewing machines with computerized functions, and the growth in the number of sewing-related sites on the Internet. If you have the ability to sew, you can offer such services as alterations, canvas repair, and antique quilt restoration, as well as sewing original creations such as customized bedding, Christmas ornaments, custom slip and chair covers, hats, Christening gowns, prom dresses, chef and barbecue outfits, swim suits, ladies' suits, soft toys and sculpture, and many more!

18. Herb farming

Today herbs are very much in demand, particularly with the popularity of specialty foods and homeopathic medicines. Many people are attracted to aromatherapy, which utilizes herbal oils and fragrances. Culinary herb varieties, such as basil, chives, parsley, oregano, thyme, mint, rosemary, and French tarragon, are growing in use. The medicinal herb ginseng, once grown in Asia is now grown in some parts of the United States and Europe, due to increase demand. The growing interest in alternative medicine and healing, both in America and the rest of the world, ensures that this is a market set to expand even further.

Small-time herb farming can be an ideal business for those who love gardening, as herbs can be grown in almost all seasons, in greenhouses, sun rooms and/or outdoors, even in relatively small spaces. Dried herbs can also be sold to crafters and florists for wreaths and floral arrangements. Your first step is to decide what area of the business you want to develop (plants, herb products, aroma-therapy, etc.). You can sell your herbs wholesale to local grocery stores and specialty food markets, or sell directly to customers on and off the Internet at retail prices. Potential clients include herbalists, aroma therapists, caterers, and restaurants specializing in gourmet cooking.

19. Party planner

If you love children and enjoy organizing parties, a party planning business may be right for you. You can assist busy parents by planning their childrens' parties, including arranging the cake, party favors and entertainment, or perhaps even doing the entertainment yourself. You can develop theme parties such as Power Rangers, 101 Dalmatians, Teletubbies, or

Pirate's Treasure. You can also offer theme menus and sell all the "fixings" for the parties (related to popular children's characters or themes) in bags that can be ordered from you in advance, containing all the decorations, favors, and even game ideas.

20. Book-keeping business

Book-keeping is a necessary evil for most business owners: they know they must maintain their records but it is a chore that many entrepreneurs would rather avoid. Business owners are often overwhelmed by business book-keeping and do not have the time to do an adequate job, and they often turn to a (reluctant) family member or friend to do this. Paying someone like you to handle their book-keeping is a smart business decision, as it allows the entrepreneur to concentrate on their business.

Book-keeping is an ideal home-based business: it requires minimal start-up costs, has high profit potential, and enjoys a steadily growing market. In addition to book-keeping principles and techniques, knowledge of basic accounting is needed. This job may be a fit for you if you have a head for numbers, computer affinity, an eye for detail and personal qualities such as trustworthiness and discretion.

21. Paid surveys

Here's an area where you can actually make money, but you have to be aware that many of the so-called paid survey opportunities advertised are either of dubious quality or are outright scams. My wife does this on occasion and has made over $80 per hour, although it sometimes requires a drive to a marketing firm's local office. That eliminates a benefit of working from home, but this job still allows for flexible work schedules (often weekends and evenings, to supplement a day job). Marketing knowledge is very valuable in this field and many consumer product companies are willing to pay well for it. But if you think you are going to be paid $100 to answer a 10 minute survey, think again. While that opportunity may exist, it's pretty rare.

22. Data entry

Although technology has brought us a long way, sometimes we have to go back to the basics. The tedious process of data entry, plugging information into a computer, is perfect for someone who wants to work from home. Often, the task is as simple as filling out a spreadsheet and emailing it back. Many legitimate firms need such work done but, as with the paid survey job, be aware that many of the data entry positions advertised on the Internet are actually opportunities to create Googe Adwords ads to sell products.

That in itself is not a problem, but this is not a work-from home job opportunity that has a confirmed wage. Instead, you would actually be hired as an affiliate marketer, selling products for which you would be paid a commission. With the Google Awords position, the problem arises because you have to use your own Adwords account. Indeed, you can make huge amounts of money as an affiliate using Adwords, but the uninitiated (and many times even the initiated) can also run up giant balances in their Adwords accounts that does not get paid by those who hired you. If you're trying to get debt-free, you really don't want a job where you could wind up in massive debt after just a month. This is a common scenario that is best to avoid.

23. Desktop publishing

Again this is a job that's perfect to do from home, but requires a specialized skill set. A strong background or skills in copy editing, writing, graphic design, and image editing are required, as is as a good computer set-up. Your job would be to create and design corporate presentations, magazine articles, books and web layouts. You should know MS Word, PowerPoint, Adobe Illustrator, Photoshop and Pagemaker, and can typically make from $15 - $40 per hour.

24. Administrative Assistant

Unlike the secretaries of yesterday, the job of today's administrative assistant encompasses all kinds of co-ordination and communications tasks. You'll schedule meetings, write memos and emails, and support executives or sales personnel. Today, all of these tasks can be done very effectively from home, thanks to the telephone, fax and Internet. Unfortunately, in most cases, you'll have to do this work during regular business hours rather than over the weekend or evenings. But there may be some flexibility. For example, if you live on the East Coast and you don't want to begin working first thing in the morning, you can recruit clients on the West Coast. Expect to receive about $12 - $18 per hour in this line of work.

19

Reduce What You Spend on Entertainment

For someone trying to cut back on expenses, one of the easiest is reducing your entertainment budget. Eating out, going to the movies, a play, opera, bar, night club, or an entertainment park with kids may be fun, but often are not as as important as paying the utility bills. However, having fun is important too, so you'll need to find ways to have fun without spending a lot. And the good news is that there are many cheap and free entertainment options, if you get creative.

1. Free concerts.

There are often free concerts, but you have to look for them. Check your local paper's entertainment section. Or search Google for your town and state, with "free concert" in quotes.

2. Rent DVDs and make popcorn.

Much cheaper than going to the movies and buying overpriced snacks, try a night at home with a good DVD and homemade popcorn.

3. Library.

One of the best forms of free entertainment around, the library contains great books, magazines, and, of course, free Internet access. Perfect for the whole family.

4. Museums.

Many museums offer free, or very inexpensive, admission one night a week.

5. Parks.

Some areas have some amazing parks, but even the most modest of areas has a place where you can go and take a quiet walk, bring the kids to a playground, or plan a picnic.

6. Board games.

This works for kids as well as adults. Stay home, have some snacks, and play some fun board games. Tired of your own games? Swap with a friend of a neighbor for a few weeks, or until you get bored of those!

7. Play a sport.

Join together with friends or gather your own family for a pick-up game of basketball, tennis competition, or any sports activity that you enjoy.

8. Skip the gym.

Forget the $40-a-month gym membership costing you almost $500 a year. Find out if the community center in your area has a free gym, or that charges a mini-mal fee. As an alternative, work out the old-fashione way: buy a good pair of running shoes or dust off the bike.

9. Crafts.

If you have kids, there are plenty of cheap but fun craft projects you can do with them that can provide hours of entertainment. The Internet is a good source of ideas.

10. Puzzles.

This will sound corny, but jigsaw puzzles can be hours of family fun. Really, try it.

11. Watch the stars.

Find a quiet, peaceful spot, preferably away from city lights, and watch the stars. Better yet, find out when the next meteor shower is, and make it a date. Shooting stars are fantastic.

12. Walk on the beach.

Mornings, evenings, and anywhere in between, a walk on the beach is one of the best forms of free entertainment in the known world. There's something mystical about the ocean, the sand, and the air.

13. Create a time capsule.

If you are a family with kids, or have a group of close friends, this can be a lot of fun. Find a box, and put mementos of things that are important to you, such as pictures, ticket stubs, newspaper clippings or programs from meaningful events. Participants should write a little entry about things going on in their lives. Seal it with a date of at least five years in the future, when you'll all open it and enjoy the gift of memories.

14. Conduct a treasure hunt.
Another corny idea that's tons of fun has one person leaving a series of clues in hidden spots. Each clue leads to another, with the final clue ending in a treasure (it doesn't have to be expensive - perhaps a bit of candy or something like that).

15. Build something.
A home project like building bookshelves, a fort, a bench, or an umbrella stand can be a lot of fun. If you don't know how to build something, look it up on the Internet and give it a try. It can be a learning experience, although I suggest that you start with something easy.

16. Purge your stuff.
OK, not everyone will find this to be fun, but every now and then I like to dedicate an afternoon to decluttering a closet or bedroom. It's so satisfying to get rid of old stuff I don't need or use anymore, and look through forgotten toys, clothes, and photographs.

17. Go to a poetry reading.

This is usually free, except for the drinks. The fun of poetry readings can be enhanced if you write a poem and join in the readings.

18. Art gallery openings.

These are often free, with free wine and hors d'oeuvres. And sometimes, there's good art and even better conversations.

19. Literary readings.

Check your paper for authors promoting their books at local bookstores. Often you can find some good authors reading excerpts from their books.

20. Book club.

Find a local book club for great literary discussion and a motivation to read good books. If none exist in your area, organize a few friends to form your own.

21. Wait until the last minute.

When it gets down to a couple hours before the performance, the theater may start selling "rush" tickets at a fraction of the price. It would rather sell the seats at a bargain than let them go empty. Consolidated discount ticket booths are popping up in cities nation-wide. Or call your favorite home-town theater to see if it offers price cuts directly to the public right before show time. Of course, there's a good chance a show will sell out. So keep your plans flexible.

22. Special Discount Days.

Many theaters, museums, galleries, zoos and parks offer special discount days, such as standing room only or pay-what-you-can nights. Some even offer free admission on certain days of the month. For performances, ask about free or drastically discounted admission to dress rehearsals.

23. Babysitting Co-op.

As any parent knows, a good chunk of any entertainment budget can be eaten up just paying the babysitter. To help cut your costs, partner with a relative, neighbor or friend and trade off watching each other's kids instead. For example, you watch their kids one Saturday evening and they watch yours the following weekend. If you usually spent $10 to $20 a week on a babysitter, you could save $560 to $1,120 per year with this kind of arrangement, while enjoying the nights out knowing that your children are in good hands.

24. Catch a matinee.

Matinees aren't just for senior citizens or little kids. You can often get cheap tickets to movies, theater productions and other shows if you attend in the early afternoon instead of the prime evening time slot.

25. Eat out during the day.

Daytime is also a good time to try out a hot new restaurant and is more affordable than evening excursions. You can get lunch-menu prices for dinner-quality entrees.

26. Go with a group.

When it comes to finding cheap entertainment, more really is merrier. Buy tickets in bulk to get a 10% (or more) discount to many exhibitions and events. Team up with friends, co-workers or relatives to get the lower rate.

27. Give the secret handshake!

As with many things in life, getting a deal on entertainment can come down to who you know. You could score discount tickets to amusement parks, sports arenas and other events through clubs and associations you belong to, such as AAA, AARP, a credit union, alumni or professional association, or even your own employer. Flash your membership card and save money. And if you're a student, always ask about discounts with your ID.

28. Go back to college.

College campuses are a treasure trove of quality entertainment options, including student musical performances, film festivals, art exhibits, theater productions, dance recitals, free lectures, sporting events and more. The best part: Many are free or incredibly inexpensive. Call or do an Internet search to find out what's going on at colleges near you.

29. Fire your video store.

Spending $5 for a movie at the corner video store can add up quickly over time. And mail-order subscription services can be costly, too, unless you watch a lot of movies every month to make the expense worth it. Instead, scope out DVD kiosks in your neighborhood or check out the selection at your local public library.

30. Share an entrée.

When eating out once, another couple introduced us to the whole concept of sharing an entrée. I don't know why we never considered this before, but it makes sense – especially since we rarely finish our individual dishes anyway. We order a dish, tell the waiter we're going to share, and they split the entrée onto two separate plates. Maybe it's my imagination, but I'm convinced restaurants increase the portions when patrons share.

31. Sign up for e-mail alerts.

The Internet is a remarkable resource for finding discounts. You can visit the websites of local restaurants and sign up for their e-mail notifications. Typically they ask for personal information such as your birthday and anniversary date and, in return, they send you coupons for free appetizers and entrées.

32. Skip the drinks and dessert.

I used to really enjoy going to restaurants, but it gets costly. If you enjoy the full package - entrée, cocktail, dessert - and multiply that by two, you've added $20 to the dinner bill, excluding the tip. Try skipping the dessert or reserving alcoholic beverages for special occasions. And if a restaurant charges a ridiculous amount for a non-alcoholic beverage, I order water.

20

How to Save on Food

Think "food" not "grocery" when you assess what you are spending to feed your family. List all the places where you buy food, including the grocery store and restaurants. But don't forget the soda machine at work, the popcorn counter at the theater, the morning coffee stop, an the bottle of water at the gas station. We buy and consume food in many locations. To save money on food, eliminate or limit all except the essentials. Think, "Do we need this or simply want it?" If you track food expenses, keep track of these incidental expenses separately: they add up.

• Cook.

Let's face it. The first way to save money on food expenses is to start cooking more by yourself. Think of it this way: if someone cooks the food for you, how is it much different than hiring a cook or a house cleaner or a lawn mower or a clothes washer? Sometimes the 'cook' is Del Monte or Kraft and the food is carried home in grocery bags. Other times, the 'cook' is McDonald's or Pepsico and is passed through drive-up windows or is delivered to your door. Always remember that the cost of that labor is included in the prices you pay.

If you are used to buying pre-cooked foods, start making the change slowly. Make it a point to cook something for every meal or at least once a day. Make soup one day, cook a roast on the weekend. Put together a grain-based salad that will last several days. If you reach a point where the fridge is stocked with homemade food, celebrate by making something special, such as brownies or muffins. The objective is to never be faced with cooking an entire meal from scratch, which is too overwhelming to contemplate at the end of a long workday. If not every day, find your own rhythm, but do cook with regularity. The less we cook at home, the more we pay someone else in order to eat. The more we cook at home, the more we save.

• Make frugal food consumption a personal challenge for you and your family.
It's you versus the food companies and yes, you're David and they're Goliath. Every time a food company takes a commodity food (think "real food," the underlying ingredients) and cuts it, cooks it and packages it, it's all to tempt you to pay several multiples for the 'added value' the company brings to a commodity product. It makes you buy more, pay more and, therefore, work more and save less.

• Get good at shopping frugally for food - a week, a dollar at a time.
Don't expect to follow all of these tips at once. But if a few make sense, copy them and work the list, one week at a time. To build confidence, start with what is known as the "low-hanging fruit", the ones that are easiest to incorporate into your own habits and practices. To make the greatest difference, determine where there's the most to save in your family finances, and work those first.

• Time is money.
So it is - and many of these tips involve getting a firm

grip on grocery expenses in order to exact the most value from the dollars spent. This means time: analyzing, comparing, tracking. Here's an example. What's the price difference between the bag of dried beans that sells for $.89 and the can of beans that sells for $.99? Just a dime? No. The bag yields 7 cups of cooked beans, $.13 per cup. The can yields 1-1/2 cups of cooked beans, $.66 per cup. The canned beans - as inexpensive as they are - are five times more expensive than dried beans. Both are protein-rich, an inexpensive source of protein. If you are watching your wallet, learn how easy is it to cook dried beans.

• **Recycle & repurpose**.

That soup last night? You made enough for lunches during the week and some for the freezer, right? That roast? There's enough for sandwiches and a casserole later in the week, yes? Is it the end of the week and all that's left are bits and pieces of more leftovers? Make another soup from it. Waste not, want not.

• **Extract all the value.**

When we splurge on bacon, save the fat in a jar in the fridge: it adds great flavor to stews and eggs. When we roast a chicken, after supper throw the carcass into a pot with sliced onion, chopped celery and a bay leaf to make chicken stock. If there's not time after supper, place the carcass in a bag and freeze it for cooking on the weekend.

• Keep a running list.

When you're running low or finished the last of a staple, add it to a running grocery list that's in a handy place, such as on the fridge door. If you shop at several places weekly, maintain individual lists for each store.

• Shop your fridge, freezer and pantry first.

Before shopping for groceries, try to find away to make meals without spending a dime. Use up that soup you made two weeks ago and froze. Turn that roast pork and leftover cheese into tortillas.

• Be careful at the grocery store.

"Just food, only food." This should be your mantra when planning meals and shopping for groceries. Only go to buy food - just food and only food. No health and beauty aids (that's 'supermarket speak' for shampoo, aspirin and other personal care items). No paper products. (Think toilet paper, plastic wrap and paper towels.) No cleaning supplies. (Think dishwashing liquid and laundry soap.) No pet food. As a reminder, call your local store what it should be: a grocery store, not a supermarket. All the other items are considerably cheaper at a big-box discount store. (Think Wal-Mart. Think Target.) If you track family expenses, separate food costs from all the other items.

• Real food.

This tip is perhaps the most important of all. To save money and be frugal grocery shoppers, this is all you should be buying. Most "real food" is one ingredient long. Lettuce. Carrots. Milk. Chicken. It hasn't been cooked and packaged by a company. It probably doesn't have a brand name and a promotion budget. And it's generally cheaper.

• Shop the priorities first.

At the grocery store, fill the cart with "real food" first. This means vegetables and fruit, protein and milk. These departments are nearly always on the outside walls of the store, which is why some people suggest to shop the perimeter. Now stop. Add up what's been spent so far. Is there money left over for the extras?

• Bypass the empty calorie aisles.

If there's money left over, avoid the temptation of spending it on non-essential commercial foods that are mostly in the center aisles and are big budget killers. Ignore potato chips, cheap pizzas, ice cream, soda, and the deli counter - especially the deli counter.

• Invest in the future.

Instead, use any leftover funds to make next week's food dollar go further. Buy essential food in bulk. (Think a big bottle of olive oil or a huge bag of brown rice.) Buy a pantry item that will enhance the taste of home-cooked food. (Think dried herbs and spices.) Purchase packaging that makes it easier to store and carry food. (Think freezer containers and portion-sized plastics.) Purchase a kitchen tool that makes it easier to cook in large quantities or to save money. (Think a slow-cooker or a Dutch oven.)

• Eyes averted, make quick forays into the middle of the store.

One processed food that delivers value is frozen vegetables. Even so, make sure to buy one-ingredient vegetables - just peas, just broccoli, just green beans, just frozen spinach. On sale, they're $1 a pound, worth stocking up on. Other real food finds worth our dollars that are in the middle aisles: frozen orange juice concentrate, canned tomatoes, bags of dried beans, bags of rice, big tubs of old-fashioned oats, flour, and sugar.

• Don't shell out for water.

It's well known that bottled water is expensive, both on our budgets and on the environment. But think of the other products that contain water: cartons of orange juice, juice boxes, cans of chicken broth, cans of cooked beans, low-fat coconut milk, jello cups, applesauce, popsicles, chicken and pork injected with 'flavoring' (think water and salt), canned soup, Kool-Aid bottles, and soda pop.

• Don't pay for salt.

Specialty spice mixes are popular, and there are dozens of them, especially during the grill season. They're also 90% salt. Instead, purchase the base herbs and spices, then make homemade spice rubs. Beware of grocery-store regular prices in the spice department. Sale prices are more reasonable, especially right before Christmas. Avoid temptation of the "huge" containers of spices at some groceries and especially at warehouse clubs. Herbs and spices have a relatively short shelf life: try to buy no more than what might be used in a year. Better yet, find a good source of high-quality spices at a spice store.

• Don't drink up your food budget.

It's easy to save money by considering - and then consciously deciding - what you drink, including coffee, cans of soda, bottled water, and even wine. Instead of buying coffee beans from a local coffee shop, you can purchase big tubs of Folgers' 100% Colombian Coffee which costs perhaps 1/10, either on sale at the grocery store or at regular price at Wal-Mart. It tastes just as good. Also consider cutting back on the quantity of bottled water and soda that you purchase. It is still worth buying one or two a year, because it's cheaper, in the long run, to have a few bottles and cans on hand for long car trips, rather than buying expensive single bottles from convenience stores.

• Pay for food, not disposable packaging.

It's so easy and inexpensive to make chocolate pudding, so why do we buy it pre-cooked in plastic containers? Buy old-fashioned (and whole grain) oatmeal, not instant oatmeal packets. Buy a bag of popcorn kernels, not ready-made popped corn or microwave popcorn. If a food is heavily packaged, chances are it's not "real food" and the price is many times higher than the commodity price of the base ingredients.

• **Pay for nutrition, not snacks.**

Some of the worst nutrition values in the grocery store? Breakfast cereal. Snack crackers. Potato chips. Taco chips. Breakfast bars. Pie crusts. Boxes of mashed and scalloped potatoes. Mac 'n' cheese. They're not good for your health and they are definitely not good for your wallet.

• **Coupons.**

Who has ever seen a coupon for broccoli? What about milk? Unfortunately, there are few if any coupons for "real food" because there are no "excess margins" (for the consumer, read "savings"). Coupons are printed only for the most highly processed foods. If we begin shopping only around the edges of the grocery store for real food, the time spent clipping and sorting coupons will soon become a big waste of time.

• **Name brands & store brands.**

Private label foods (also called "store" brands or

"white label" brands) are usually less expensive and - often but not always - of the same or acceptable quality as name-brand products. Keep notes on what's good and what's not.

• Carry a calculator & a shopping notebook.
Okay, sorry, this is admittedly a little nerdy but unless you're a math whiz in your head, the calculator will figure out unit costs and help you make decisions between brands. The notebook will make it easier to track the sources and prices of the foods purchased most often. Be organized.

• For easier comparison, think price per pound.
For all foods, not just meat, and for the edible portion of the food. For example, chicken thighs and chicken legs are often sold for half or less the price of boneless chicken breasts. Are they worth it? (Nearly always, by the way, they are.)

• Watch prices and price tags with an eagle eye.
We're in a rush, we've got our list, it's oh-so-easy to just toss food into the grocery cart. Watch out for tricks, such as items on sale at the entry to the produce department, while further in a similar variety at regular

price may actually cost less than the "sale price." Remember to compare the prices of different types of apples, for example, and look for size differentials: a gallon of bleach may cost $1.54 while a half gallon is priced at $1.34.

Supermarkets may also be sloppy about placing price signs. A price tag for store-brand butter may be placed above a premium brand; offering apples for "$10 for 10 lbs" right next to oranges priced at "$10 for 10" - this works out as $.50 an apple versus $1.00 an orange.

• Loose versus bags.

On occasion, packaging pays. Bags of onions, apples and lemons are often less expensive than individual onions, apples and lemons - so long as you can use them all.

• Explore world cuisines.

If you learn about Vietnamese, Mexican and other international cuisines, you will discover that meat is a Western luxury. Our meat portions are huge. Many recipes call for a three-pound roast to serve four or five people, or four chicken breasts to serve four people. In contrast, the standard that the USDA uses is that a pound of meat serves four. This means that a chicken breast, which these days can weigh 8 to 10 ounces, should add up to 2 to 2-1/2 servings. But in these non-Western cookbooks, a pound of meat will serve eight or even ten. Meat is used as an accent, rather than as the primary staple.

• International groceries.

Small ethnic groceries often offer prices considerably lower than U.S. supermarkets, especially for ingredients authentic to that particular cuisine.

• Know your staples.

If your family goes through a dozen yogurt cups in a week, invest in an inexpensive yogurt maker. If hot popcorn is an evening ritual, learn how to make popcorn in a saucepan - and once you have homemade popcorn, homemade caramel corn is just a few minutes away. Ice cream? A commercial ice cream maker may seem like $50 that doesn't need spending. But homemade ice cream is made only from cream, eggs, sugar and flavoring, all "real foods", and is easy to make at home for much less. What about bread for sandwiches and to fill out a light meal like soup or eggs? With bread at $3 or $4 a loaf now, a bread machine may be an investment worth considering.

• Eat in season.

For example, mid-winter, blueberries are imported from somewhere and cost the equivalent of $10 a pint. In July, when blueberries are imported from a couple of states away, the regular price will be $3. You can also find excellent produce (though not usually quite as picture perfect as at the grocery store) from produce dealers selling at an outdoor weekly market.

• Know what's on sale and whether it's really a good deal.

Sometimes what may be on sale at one store is actually more than the regular price at another. Pay attention to the prices and determine if you are actually getting a good deal.

• Consistent pricing.

Even better, identify a grocery source whose prices are consistently low. For example, my nearby supermarket will occasionally sell chicken breasts for $2 a pound in five-pound containers, presumably to compete with warehouse-type stores. But seven weeks out of eight, chicken breasts sell for $6 a pound. If you find a grocery where your most-used cuts of meat - chicken breasts, pork tenderloin, and roasts - are priced the same, week in and week out, it may be worth making a trip once a month and then freezing the meat.

• Warehouse clubs.

The prices at warehouse clubs like Sam's Club and Costco are tempting. Trouble is, "real food" is relatively rare along those long, tall aisles and often in such large quantities that there's a large risk of waste. Still, for many families, warehouse clubs provide real value.

• Grow your own.

If you have a few pots and a small garden, you can grow enough garlic for the year, an abundance of fresh herbs and, perhaps even a bumper crop of rhubarb. From $10 worth of plants you can yield $100 of savings. Imagine the value derived from growing much of your own produce during the summer, and preserving it for the long winter.

• Watch the register.

In most grocery stores, advertised sales change every week, so the scanners have to be updated constantly.

Surprisingly, they are often not, and you get charged the full amount, rather than the discounted price. To get the deal you're after, keep an eye on the price being registered by the scanner at the check-out counter. Put all the week's specials in a corner of your cart and line them up on the check-out counter together so you can easily keep track of the prices you're being charged.

• **Don't assume that regular-priced items are being entered correctly either.**
After all, the person at the register may not know a pomegranate from a persimmon. It is worthwhile to check that the cashier is entering the correct product code, especially for different types of produce which are hard to tell apart or have names which are easily confused.

• **Collect your payoff if there's a mistake.**
Many people don't know it, but big chains like Giant, Safeway, and Kroger will often give you an item for free if the scan shows a higher price than what's advertised. (Tobacco, alcohol, pharmacy items, and dairy are excluded.) Before you leave the store, do a quick scan of the receipt and look for any incorrectly

charged items.

• Be persistent.

If your grocer runs out of an advertised special, ask customer service for a rain-check - a written promise to sell you the item at the lower price when it's restocked. Make sure the slip specifies the maximum number you can buy for the sale price (usually six). Ask about the time limit for using your rain-check (it's usually 15 days).

Don't be fooled by deals like two for $1. You don't have to buy two. If the ad says "Buy two for $5" and you want only one, you can still get it for $2.50, unless the sale sign notes otherwise. If the item doesn't automatically scan that way, point out the sale price to the cashier.

• Weigh before you pay.

If you're buying a 10-pound bag of potatoes, put it on the scale before you put it in your cart. Many items weigh less than what the package says.

• Stock up, but wisely.

Before you stash 10 boxes of something on your shelves, check the sell-by date. Even seemingly ageless products like tea bags and toothpaste eventually expire, and you don't want to be throwing out eight unopened packages when that happens!

21

How To Keep Your Job in a Bad Economy

Abad economy can very quickly become a "very bad economy" if you lose your job. And it seems that everyone's job is on the line these days. With the way things have been going so far during this recession, I thought it was worthwhile to post these suggestions which originally came from the *Wall Street Journal* but really are common sense. These are basic but valuable suggestions which can help you improve your chances of keeping your job:

- Make yourself indispensable.
- Don't be high-maintenance.
- Stay busy.
- Do damage control.

Here's my two cents:

1. **Focus on performance.**
Those who deliver results (sales, cost savings, new customers, etc.) will be the last to go.

2. **Have a good attitude.**
Strong performers with bad attitudes are fired before strong performers with good attitudes.

3. **Damage Control.**
If you have a sense that you may be let go, do what they suggest and "do damage control." For instance, you could offer to take a lower salary, be hired back as a consultant, take on more tasks, etc. - anything to make your cost-per-output go down.

Is your company cutting back? Are lay-offs the current topic making the rounds in the office? Do you feel uncertain about things because you are not part of the "in" group? Would you feel better moving up a rung on the ladder and getting out of the danger zone?

There is a way to move into the comfort zone in your organization and avoid those lay-offs. You can move into the "unofficial" power group that the real power group in your organization relies on to get things done. And it is not that hard. Here are three simple tips recommended by organization expert James J. Heaphey.

1. Give yourself a quiz with just one question. How easy would it be for someone else to do my job? Grade yourself on a scale of 1 to 10. If you come up with an 8 or less, start doing something extra that lends an extra dimension to your job. If you can't come up with uniqueness or relevancy, do something extra for your manager. Make life better for him or her. Make yourself invaluable so that if you left, life would be more difficult for your manager. This will create a friend who will go to bat for you.

2. Jockey to get situated near the power center. A cubbyhole or desk near the center of action is better than a paneled office in Siberia. Being "in the right place at the right time." is sometimes being the first person the CEO sees when he needs something done quickly. It may also place you in a position to overhear plans being made for programs in which you might be able to fit in.

3. Be seen and heard.

Be visible. Try to find extra work that will be seen, or at least that people will see you doing it. When others shy away from doing extra work, seize it as an opportunity. It could be an audition for something bigger. It will make a favorable impression on decision-makers too. You will be viewed as a more valuable person, one worthy of consideration for better things

Security is a happy thing. For some it is a consistent cash flow and eight hours of sleep at night. If you are employed in an organization of any size and are threatened by the axe falling, by following the few ideas outlined, you may not only hold off the axe-man but you may find the security you are craving.

• Survive!

Survival in any environment is often the result of intelligent adjustments rather than sheer luck. Adjusting, by making yourself visible, is letting the company power players know that you have value and they can use it to their advantage. In his book *"How to Survive in an Organization"*, author James J. Heaphey, an organization expert who has consulted for such corporate giants as GE and IBM, shows the reader the reality of functioning in a large organization or corporation.

Recession and inflation have combined to introduce us to the new-fangled term "stagflation", which means when costs are soaring but jobs are hard to come by. In such a scenario, most people are considering themselves lucky that they have a job to call their own and a salary that helps put food on the table and takes care of other basic necessities. It's at times like these that care has to be taken to hold on to your livelihood; a lackadaisical attitude could see you on the wrong end of a lay off. If that does happen and you become collateral damage in the blink of an eye, you have no one to blame but yourself.

The process of holding on to your job and making sure that you leave only on your terms starts not when there are rumors of pay cuts and lay offs circulating on the company grapevine, but the very day you start your job as a new employee. Here are a few pointers that offer guidance in helping you keep your job even as heads are rolling around you:

• Give your best from day one, and continue to do so even though you think your position is well-established.

• Create the impression that you are a team player first and foremost, and that you consider the company's goals higher than your personal ones.

• Strive to improve your performance in each task that you undertake. If you settle for mediocrity, there's no way you're going to push yourself to work harder and reach higher levels.

• Do things when they are meant to be done instead of putting them off until the last minute. Be cautious not to run late on tasks that have a definite deadline. Even if you've done a good job, a job completed late has lost its value.

•Take time to mentor a junior staff member even though there's nothing in it for you. Your superiors will notice that you're helping your colleagues and teaching them the right way to go about their work.

•Be sincere in all dealings with your co-workers and your superiors. Even if there are aspects to your job that you don't like, talk to your manager or supervisor instead of complaining about it to the rest of the office.

•Do not indulge in office gossip, especially about the "higher ups".

•Never rat out on colleagues. Play the ignorant game and do not point fingers even if you know who was responsible, unless someone else is unfairly taking the blame.

•Offer to take on new and challenging assignments that test and improve your skills regularly.

•Invest in furthering your education, even earning a degree or diploma, that will help you - whether you stay in the same company or move on.

•In the event of a lay-off, offer to take a pay-cut if your company will keep you on the payroll.

•Most companies are hesitant to fire employees who

are loyal, hard working and willing to improve. So make sure you're on this list, long before the rumblings start and the heads start to roll.

22

How to Find a Job If You've Been Laid Off

The most important secret of successful job hunting after you have been laid off is to treat the unpleasant task as a job. Since you are no longer working, you have the time to dedicate to your job search. If you spent 7 hours a day working, you should spend 7 hours a day with your job hunt. The more hours that you put into looking for a job after a lay off, the faster you will find your next job.

Don't procrastinate. If you worked 50-hour workweeks in your cramped cubicle, you should spend

60 on your couch-based job search. For now, your new job is 40 hours a week looking for employment; keep busy at it and don't let yourself get down.

Try to establish and keep a routine. It is important to sniff out any opportunities fast, since new jobs may be frozen now.

It's easier to find a job when you have a job, so see if you can negotiate to stay at your office for a finite period of time or be given a workspace from which to conduct your job search. Ask the company to keep you on the payroll until you've used up vacation time, PTO, or sick time. This way you can legitimately say you are currently employed. Similarly, negotiate a severance package that includes extended health insurance and other benefits. If needed, hire a good labor lawyer to help you with this.

By working towards getting a new job, you bring structure and discipline to your life and you'll feel better about yourself because you're taking control of your situation. Stay busy and keep your mind off your current state of unemployment. The results will pay off in no time.

Post your resume on every large job board on the Internet. Start with Monster, Dice, Career Builder, TheLadders, an Net-temps. Then do a Google search on job listings to find all the smaller or regional job boards. Many ignore the smaller sites after being laid off. Don't make that mistake.

Do not stop with just posting your resume. Make a daily practice of searching the listings on each job board and responding to jobs that look like a great fit. It is important to run your searches every day so that when a new job appears, you will be among the first to apply. Remember that most people go job searching after being laid off so the market can be rather competitive. It pays to be first in line.

Next, take out your resume and rewrite it. You will want to start by updating all of your contact information. Add in the information about the job that you were just laid off from. Make sure that you highlight any specialized training and education that you have received. These pieces of informational will be vital to your job hunt.

It's crucial to make a tracking form for all of your job hunt activities. You will use this form to track all of the efforts that you make while searching for your next job. This form will help you remember all of the places that you applied to, so you can follow up.

Research the niche that you would like to work in. You can use many different methods to research job openings. Internet and newspaper ads are the most popular ways to research job openings. Prepare for your next interview thoroughly. Then you'll stand out during the interview and know what you're getting into if you take the job.

You will want to apply to seven to ten job openings a day. Job hunting is a numbers game. Of the jobs that you apply to, the odds are that possibly 10% of them will call you in for an interview. To increase your chance of getting an interview after you have been laid off, you want to make sure that you continuously apply to jobs throughout the time that you are laid off. Remember that the job search is a numbers game. There's something called the "Rule of 21" in job hunting. For every 21 contacts you make, you'll get one positive response (not necessarily an offer but perhaps an interview or request for more information). This means you need to cast your net wide and call in any favors that might be due to you.

Where to look for a job: Remember your limits. If you're a programmer in Washington DC, don't bother applying for the postal position in Detroit. Pick an industry and geographical area and stick with it. Make a long list of industries, and organizations within those industries, where you could put your skills and experience to use. Don't worry too much about who might be hiring; instead, develop a lengthy list of potential employers, even companies you don't want to work for. The reason to include less desirable companies in your search is to put yourself in a stronger negotiating position in the event one of those firms wants you.

Though the Internet is an invaluable resource for researching companies, it's not the best medium for submitting job applications and resumes. If you can do it, at least a million other people can do it, too. You can utilize the Internet, including Monster Board, Craig's List, and even Yahoo Jobs, but prioritize your time by using your network to make contact with hiring managers inside the companies where you're interested in working. Headhunters and search firms may yield little help in landing you a new job, since these work best in an up economy, when there's competition for labor. Instead of spending a day meeting with them, use your time to attend a conference or networking event, where you have the opportunity to make personal connections.

Make a list of every company you would like to work for. Try to put together at least 30 - 50 names, and the larger the business the better. Then check the job listings on each corporate web page at least once a week. Most large firms post new job openings on their corporate web site as they become available. You should keep adding companies to your weekly list until you find that you have at least 10 new openings to peruse every week .

When you find a job opening that interests you, fill out an on-line application and submit your resume. Then record the job title, job number or identifier, the date you applied, and the phone number of the Human Resources Department on your tracking form. You will need this information when you call the Human Resources Department to follow up on your application. When you call, ask if your application has been forwarded to the hiring manager, whether he/she has provided any feedback, and if there are any other job openings for which you might be qualified. One of the advantages of being laid off is that you have lots of time available to you. Use that time well.

Make a list of everyone you know who works at a company that might offer the type of job for which you are seeking. Send each person on this list a copy of your resume and ask if they are aware of any openings at the company where they work. Then ask them if they have friends at other companies that might know of an opening. This kind of networking is important because many jobs get filled before they are ever advertised, as somebody knew someone who was available.

Since you might be out of practice in job interviewing, you must prepare yourself. Write down five reasons you shouldn't be hired. Then write rebuttals and memorize them. Use them in an interview to plead your case. Practice bragging. Also, in 90 seconds, describe who you are, your best skills, who you've worked for and what you intend to do next. It's called the elevator pitch. Become good at it.

Another step to take in the job application process is "dress to impress". Sometimes, your clothing can say it all. Companies are looking for a good fit, and many times people are not hired because something conveys that you would stand out at the company. It could have nothing to do with your capability. Interview the interviewers by asking questions that give you a feel for how good a match you are for the company and vice versa.

Stop reading about the economy (unless you are an out-of-work economist). Job seekers should not spend their time listening to too much news about the economy because the news is so bad. It discourages people when they need to stay optimistic. Discouragement is the biggest obstacle to finding a new job. What's more, prospective employers can sense discouragement and negativity in candidates, and it turns them off. If they sense that you're negative or in a panic, they're much less likely to think that you're a good candidate. They want someone who's resilient. They don't want an employee who will hurt morale. So stay proud, and keep your chin up.

23

How to Manifest
Money and Success

After you've been laid off, you feel vulnerable. When you feel vulnerable, it's easy to second - guess yourself and to sink into depression. It's difficult to resist those negative thoughts. But for your own well-being and the success of your job search, you have to.

Instead of dwelling on all the reasons why your employer might have selected you for a pink slip, always remember that the fundamental reason you lost your job was because your employer was having trouble competing during this economic downturn, not because you're a bad worker.

Remember that lots of other talented, hard-working professionals are getting laid off and you can still be a valuable employee at another company. There are still plenty of companies that are in desperate need of quality employees. There is something else out there for you, and chances are, it's a great opportunity that will improve your future.

I think it is safe to say that most of the world needs money to survive, although not everyone has a healthy view of it. Many religions teach that money is the "root of all evil". They hold on to clichés such as, "The rich are getting richer while the poor are getting poorer."

Abundance is about living in optimal health, vibrancy, and purpose with resources. It is about empowering relationships and having a strong sense of our true self. Material wealth and riches are a manifestation of mental and spiritual wealth that lies within the individual. As a result of this spiritual and mental wealth, one can help manifest material wealth and turn it into material riches.

We should not concern ourselves with the fear

that material wealth will corrupt us. Material wealth, including money, will only enhance what you already are. If you have good character and compassion for others, with material wealth you will have more good character and greater compassion for others. If you are a scoundrel and a cheat, with material wealth you will be an even bigger scoundrel and a bigger cheat. Therefore, if you are kind, giving, loving, and creative, with your wealth you will be even more kind, giving, loving, and creative while enjoying a life of abundance. If you are insecure, selfish, hoarding, and deceitful, with your wealth, you will be even more insecure, selfish, hoarding, and deceitful while living a life of discontent, sadness, and self-destruction.

Some people fear abundance because they believe that abundance will require hours and hours of hard work. The Universal Law of Economy of Force or the Principle of Least Resistance contends that this is just not true. Too many people are spending 16 hour days working, hoping that soon all their money troubles will end and they can retire in the Bahamas at 65 years old.

Unfortunately, this is not happening. Recent studies show that many people have been forced to come out of retirement. There is a reality check we should cash long before we cash our pay check and this reality check is...We are not supposed to work hard. What? That's right. We are supposed to work creatively. That's what the human spirit desires.

Hard work causes mental and spiritual fatigue that will subsequently make mental and spiritual wealth impossible. If we have no mental and spiritual wealth, then we have nothing to show for all our hard work. This fatigue is also the result of our own resistance. Because of this resistance, we interrupt the flow of abundance in our lives and prevent ourselves from being able to create. The truth is we create in our thoughts. When we are mentally fatigued, our thought process does not work properly.

In our world of thoughts, when we are relaxed and comfortable, the Universe whispers plans, inventions, and ideas, which are waiting for our higher consciousness to receive them. This is the abundance within us at work. By stilling the mind through meditation, we discover this knowledge and wisdom as we allow our creative energy to flow. When we act on it, we create a kind of wealth. Each of these plans, inventions, and ideas serve a purpose, which is to help humanity in some impacting way. Hence, there is already a demand for your idea. There are millions of people wanting it. All you need is the faith and courage to execute your plan.

As this creative energy continues to flow, your execution will seem effortless, particularly when you take the time to think it through and determine how each step should be carried out. Before long, you will have tapped into the field of infinite possibilities. You will have opened the flood gates to wealth and success and you will have embarked on the journey to living abundantly.

A second group of individuals who fear abundance is often classified as fearing success. Amazingly, there are more who fear success than any other group of people who fear abundance. These individuals have had personal experiences where they felt responsible for everyone else. This often happens in a family or group dynamic where the individual feels thatsuccess will cause him or her to have to carry the entire family or group. Because this burden is overwhelming, the individual fears success and settles for mediocrity. While this would be classified as a fear of success, there is another category of those who fear abundance.

The third group that fears abundance would be classified as those who fear failure. Again, the Principle of Expectations contends that energy follows thoughts. Therefore, keep thinking it and it will happen...whatever it is. Here is a novel thought: Practice the Universal Law of No Attachments. Under this law, you go through the process doing all you can while the Universe handles the details.

All you have to do is what you know how to do. You stay in meditation, asking the Universe to show you what you should do next. After you have done it, step back and let the Universe handle the rest. If the Universe says write a book, it will present you with opportunities to learn what you need to do to write a book. Then you can write the book without worrying about how many copies will sell or whether the audience will like it.

Simply do what you know how to do. Meditate. Allow the flow. Expect the best. Gain wisdom in what you are doing. Take each step expecting the best and the best will come. That is abundance in action.

If you want more money in your life, then you've got to show "money love". This may sound strange to you, but the Law of Attraction simply stated says "Like attracts like." Attracting money into your life is much like a love relationship.

If you want to attract that sexy woman or that handsome guy into your life, then you call them on the phone. You meet together on a dinner date. Perhaps you write love letters or sweet poems. You find out what the person likes and make a little surprise gift. You keep a picture of that person in your wallet. You are in love. This is basically what the law of attraction is about. It's not just saying or writing affirmations. It's not just using pictures to visualize things. It's putting your whole heart, soul and mind into it.

With money, it has to be the same way. Below are the initial steps to attracting money:

1. Realize money is like electricity. In and of itself, it is not good or evil. Much like electricity, you can use it to do a lot of good or to cause a lot of unhappiness. Many people blame money for their mistakes and are afraid to face responsibility for their own life.

2. Everything that you want to manifest requires a specific spirituality; spirituality means an intense feeling for something. It is a healthy and balanced love for something. If you are afraid to love money, how can you ever expect it to want to come to you? Remember, this is a healthy and balanced love.

3. Keep pictures or symbols of money to help you

focus and remind you of your intention. You can use pictures of money, real money, or symbols such as rocks or marbles. Use whatever works best for you.

4. Take action. Don't just take action for action's sake; rather, meditate and think it through. Trust your subconscious to lead you to do the right action, but don't expect things to just fall out of the sky and into your lap.

5. Imagine. Use your imagination to focus on what you would feel like if you were wealthy. Exactly how much money would you like to have? When? Make it crystal clear into your mind and then work with the feeling of already having it now. I recommend this should be done on a daily basis for at least half an hour, but again, do what works best for you. Remember that you want to do this regularly and you want this to be a fun thing, not a chore.

To attract money, you have to become a money magnet. You do so through the process of magnetization. The physical means of obtaining wealth is through setting up businesses and systems that bring in money. The metaphysical process of magnetization is what brings in more sales and revenue when all other factors are left unchanged. It is the very thing that makes the difference in results among people with similar actions.

Two people that take the same physical actions to create wealth may obtain significantly different results because of what each is doing metaphysically. The universe is mental and therefore you can affect reality greatly through the use of the imagination. The rich are able to get more results with less effort and in an easier way because they do more of their work mentally than physically. Wealth consciousness is what imbues all your action with prosperous effect. There are different ways of mental work.

Imagine money coming to you. Visualize and feel yourself as a center of attraction where money is flowing to you from all directions. Imagine a shower of hundred dollar bills falling from the sky, onto you, in your room and all around your home. Imagine there is such a flood of abundance that everyone is basking in, with more than enough for everybody. Feel the joy and happiness of having enough money to do whatever you want. This imagery fills your subconscious with wealth.

A recent popular movie, *The Secret*, is a testament to the Law of Attraction. Essentially, it states that whatever you think about, you attract to you. Think about and dwell on prosperity, and you'll attract more. Conversely, if you have thoughts centered on poverty or limited means, then that is the realm in which you'll dwell.

If you are a fan of personal development courses, books and seminars, you probably would know that the greatest success and personal development coaches - such as Brian Tracy, Bob Proctor and Anthony Robbins - talk about positive affirmations to manifest money, wealth, health or whatever is desired. Is it true that you can manifest anything that you desire? "It's not the events of our lives that shape us, but our beliefs as to what those events mean," said Anthony Robbins.

So what are affirmations? Why are affirmations so powerful? Affirmations are statements of acceptance that you use to allow the manifestation of your desires - be they money, love, health or anything else. Affirmations are powerful, positive thoughts and statements sent out by you to the Universe.

To practice positive affirmations, you will need to eliminate negative thoughts in your mind, in speech, and even in your actions. You must believe that you alone can have your destiny and desires manifested. It must be a positive, powerful belief with unwavering faith. Combining positive affirmations together with creative visualizations, you can create and manifest abundance in your life.

If your desire is to attract money easily, then your affirmation may be as follows: "I manifest money easily and effortlessly." Repeat it several times while believing that you are already manifesting money. Start to visualize that money is already flowing to you and that you already have the wealth that you desire. Feel as though it has already happened. While in this mental condition, keep yourself open to all ways and means in which money can flow into your life. It is important that the affirmations you feel are appropriate for you. The affirmations must resonate with you or charge you emotionally.

Here are some manifesting money and wealth affirmations. It is better for you to compose your own affirmations because then you will relate to them better and feel them more strongly:

•I am receiving creating wealth now.

•I have an abundance of whatever I desire.

•All my needs are being met now and I am grateful.

•I have unlimited money and wealth.

•I now give and receive freely.

You must believe in your affirmations for them to work. Frame your affirmations only in the present tense because you are creating your future, while framing them in the future tense shows a lack of confidence, and your affirmations may never materialize. Do not get impatient and expect to see immediate results, although that may happen. Usually it takes time to change you and your situation.

Affirmations are futile if they fail to reach you deeply enough to touch the limitless powers of your subconscious mind. Now that you know how to use affirmation, use it often to manifest money, wealth and other positive desires into your life.

In order for an individual to have a prosperity mindset, they need to be focused. It is possible for people to get what they desire if they are single-minded in their pursuit, and do not allow negative thoughts to interfere with their goal.

In most circumstances, however, this is easier said than done, and we all allow other people and situations to dictate how we think and how we feel. In doing this we allow outside forces to control us. If you want to have a prosperity mindset, you need to recognize that you are in control. If you are not, then you need to take control - of your finances, your passions, and of your mind. When you have control of your mind, you have control of your life.

If you want more out of life then you must first become more. As Jim Rohn says, "To have more, be more." You must work harder on yourself than you do on your job.

The idea of creating a prosperity mindset has been around for some time. It has been nicely elucidated by many experts in the field, including James Allen, Napoleon Hill, Randy Gage, Bob Proctor, Joe Vitale, and Bob Doyle. Allen's book, *As a Man Thinketh*, is a classic, offering a basic premise that it's not the events that control your life, but your reaction to those events, and you control that reaction.

One key component stressed by many of these experts for the development of this prosperity mindset is the recognition that others have been very successful and that you can follow their example in the steps taken.

1. It is important for every individual to look at the success of others. To examine it and to see what made them a success. This is especially important if they

are in a field or an area of interest that you would like to get into. This allows the individual to see someone succeed in that field or area or interest, and reassure you that success is possible.

2. Seeing an individual being successful in a field of interest to you will provide you with positive reinforcement that success can be achieved.

3. Studying individuals who are successful gives you the chance to emulate what they have done and possibly follow in their footsteps. It is important to read up on successful people's lives and see how they overcame obstacles to get where they are today.

4. In order to achieve a prosperity mindset, you should surround yourself with successful individuals. This allows their habits, actions, beliefs and thoughts to rub off on you in a positive way. Likewise, you must cut yourself free from those who are constantly mired in negative thoughts. Basically do what you must to rid yourself of the energy-sapping vampires in your life. Wave some garlic if you think it will keep them at bay!

5. After doing these things, you need to take stock of what you are currently doing, and see if it matches the things you should be doing to achieve prosperity.

6. If you want to lead a happy, healthy, and prosperous life, then you must accept first that this can be your destiny. Once you are able to recognize and believe in that premise, you too can enjoy that life. At that point it comes down to creating and working a smart plan to accomplish that goal.

There are millions of people in this world; what makes some people more prosperous than others? There are a variety of factors, but your attitude plays a big part. There are a number of things you can do to develop a prosperity mindset in addition to studying the example of successful people in your field:

1. As mentioned previously, search out and model the success stories of others, especially as they pertain to your industry. Know that there are many others who have become extremely successful doing what you want to do.

2. Take a super-successful person in your industry

to lunch and pick their brain. Ask them for recommendations on how you can be successful and request contacts of those who might help you succeed.

3. Cultivate a relationship with a successful mentor.

4. Create a network of successful, prosperous friends with positive attitudes.

5. Create a team of professionals dedicated to helping you succeed.

6. Practice positive prosperity affirmations.

7. Get in the habit of seeing opportunity everywhere - it is!

8. Create multiple streams of income.

9. Don't undertake too much at once. Focus on one great money-making system and develop it. Get it running well before developing another.

10. Project an image of super-success and wealth, and you will attract more of the same.

11. Give generously to others. Give your time, money, advice, and help. It will return magnified and multiplied.

Those who go into any project with a prosperity mindset expect to succeed. And those who expect to succeed and do everything in their power to make it happen stand a much better chance of actually succeeding. The confidence and power that you project to others in your ideas or products are often reflected back to you. Believe in your product and others will too. Believe in yourself and others will too.

Realize that your true wealth comes from within, and that you are prosperous regardless of the externals. Be totally responsible for everything that happens in your life even if you don't think you are. Treat yourself and others as individuals of importance and success and you will be treated in the same manner. Carry yourself with a prosperity mindset and look for opportunities for personal and financial growth at every turn. You will find them.

24

How To Invest In
Real Estate

In general, real estate is an exciting and lucrative way to create sustainable wealth and residual income, while securing your family's economic future. Unlike many other business opportunities, real estate entrepreneurs don't need a mountain of cash or flawless credit in order to get in the game.

Most people think that profiting from real estate (other than becoming a realtor) is about selling or renting property. But there are other options, or variations of these options, that can help you make money from real estate.

It is well-known that during difficult economic times, real estate values drop. But real estate generally operates in cycles – sometimes the value of a property is high and sometimes it is low. If the prices are dropping now, at some point they are likely to increase. So it is worthwhile to buy when the prices are good, and then wait for the property to appreciate. And remember, if your property's value decreases during rough times, that is also an opportunity for you to benefit financially – with the tax deductions!

You should take the initiative in finding real estate opportunities. For example, on your way to the supermarket, you may pass properties that clearly show neglect. Lawns haven't been mowed? Flowers haven't been watered? Shutters falling off the hinges? House hasn't been painted in years? Perhaps the property needs a new landlord, or the house is approaching foreclosure. Maybe the landlord is elderly or passed away and the heirs don't have time to worry about the property. You can obtain the current owner's name and contact information through your city government. This is an ideal opportunity to try and purchase a property at a bargain price!

Sometimes you have to be creative with property. For example, if you want to profit more from the real estate you own, think about changing its use – either for more potential in selling it (or selling it at a higher price) or for renting it. A basement could be turned into an office, a 2-storey house could be converted into a Bed 'n Breakfast, and apartments could be turned into a condominium. Keep in mind any relevant zoning laws that you would have to incorporate or any community approval you would need to receive.

Do you own property that you rent out? Make sure you are keeping your costs down and earning as much as you can from the property. For example, if you are paying for the utilities, make sure that you are using fluorescent light bulbs (which cost more to buy but last long and keep your electric bills down), or ensure that you have proper sealing by windows to keep cold air out in the winter (and therefore keep the heating bills down).

Keep track of the rents in the area; when mortgages are hard to get there may be many more people wanting to rent properties, so rents can actually rise when times are tough. You can also charge separate fees for additional benefits on the rental property, such as a driveway for parking or a garage.

Some city governments have established programs to beautify their city and bring residents to areas that may be more run-down. They often will offer abandoned homes for sale at a give-away price (sometimes even as low as $1), and in return will demand a commitment from you to invest a certain amount of money to fix up the property to make it more appealing so that it can be re-sold for a higher price. If you are handy with with tools, many of the repairs can be done yourself, to cut down costs, or you can find people with time on their hands who will agree to fix up the house at low prices. Then you will be entitled to re-sell the home at costs appropriate for the renovated structure and make a profit for yourself.

Many people make it a hobby to buy and fix up properties, moving in and working on it in their spare time and selling up every year, ready to start again with a new dilapidated home. Your family has to be willing to live with a certain amount of disruption and to pick up and move frequently, but if you factor in the costs of repairs and redecorating, as well as the legal costs of buying and selling, there is money to be made if you enjoy renovation work.

Beyond the selling or renting, here are six

effective strategies for launching your own real estate investing empire:

1. Bird–Dogging.

This is probably one of the simplest ways of getting started as a real estate investor. Instead of marketing property, you're more of an information broker. A bird-dog simply locates property that is available at below-market prices, gathers some information about the property and the owner, and forwards the information to a real estate investor who is willing to make the purchase.

Bird-dogs gather much of the information that a real estate investor needs in order to evaluate whether or not a property would make a good investment. Examples of the kind of information gathered include:

- Name and address of property owner.
- Asking price of the property.
- Condition of property (sometimes with photographs).
- Information about current financing and payment status.
- Background information regarding liens and other encumbrances.
- Report about owner's motivation to sell.

• Sometimes an analysis of rehabilitation costs and anticipated after repair value.

Depending on the arrangement you work out with the investor and the amount of work involved, bird-dog fees average between $500 and $1000, and sometimes much more. You don't need any cash or credit and, because you're simply providing another investor with information, there's absolutely no risk to you of becoming entangled in any type of property dispute. You risk only your time, and if the investor to whom you give the information fails to pay you for your services, you simply avoid doing business with them again in the future. However, investors are hungry for money-making properties, so the overwhelming majority will gladly pay you for quality information.

2. Wholesaling.

This method of real estate investing involves many of the same elements of bird-dogging, but in this case, you actually approach the owner of the property, negotiate a sale price, and place the property under contract for sale. Instead of making the purchase yourself, however, you assign - or sell - your interest in the property to another investor, who then completes the transaction in your place.

For instance, pretend you locate a property worth $100,000 and you were able to negotiate a sales price with the owner of $60,000. You would gather all the required information, and "sell" your real estate contract to another investor. That investor will generally be willing to pay you between $1,000 and $3,000 for the right to complete the transaction with the seller in your place. Again, the amount of money you can make for each transaction will vary depending upon the investor with whom you are working and the amount of work you have invested in the process. I've heard of investors receiving as much as $5,000-$10,000, depending on the margin of profit available to the investor.

3. Double Closing.

Sometimes you'll locate a property that has an extremely motivated owner. If you do, it's possible that the seller might be willing to sell you the property for as little as 40% of its value. If this happens, you can still assign your contract to another buyer, but you may want to keep more of the profit for yourself. When this is the case, you simply arrange for a double closing. Here's how it works:

• You sign a contract to purchase the property from the seller.

• You then sign a contract to sell the property to another buyer or investor.

• On closing day, the investor or buyer of the property pays you for your interest in the property.

• You then take the proceeds you've received from the sale of the property to pay the seller, retaining the difference for yourself.

Because there is an increased risk that your buyer could potentially back out of the deal before the transaction is complete, you receive a much greater reward. Another way of accomplishing the same goal is by obtaining a loan in order to first pay the seller for the property. You can then turn around and sell your interest in the property to another buyer. While you'll incur some financing charges to the money lender, you may determine that the expense is worth it, in light of the amount of money you'll be making off of the deal.

4. Subject to Finance.

The fourth strategy I want to suggest for getting involved in real estate investing with little cash or credit is purchasing a property from a seller subject to financing. You don't have to actually assume legal responsibility for the existing financing, but you purchase from the seller and acknowledge the existence of the current financing.

Each month, you would pay the owner of the property a house payment equal to the amount you've worked out, and the homeowner will then make the underlying mortgage payment, retaining the difference for themselves.

If the owner's lender finds out that equitable title of the property has passed to you, there is an outside chance that the lender could call the note and require payment in full for the loan. However, the reality is that right now, millions of Americans are unable to make their house payments. Lenders are overwhelmed by foreclosures and other delinquencies. They don't have the time or the inclination to look at each payment check that comes through the door to ensure that the payment is actually being made by the borrower. In all honesty, they're just grateful to get their money; they really don't care how the loan gets paid as long as it gets paid.

5. No Money Down Deals.

Many people ask whether it is really possible to buy real estate with no money down, particularly mortgage brokers and realtors. Since mortgage brokers are, by definition, trained to fund a loan based on bank requirements like 20% down payments, anything else seems to be beyond the scope of their possibilities. Many real estate professionals don't seem to understand the concept of "no money down deals."

First, the definition of no money down does not mean "no money down". It simply means none of your money down. It could be Uncle Bob's money, the seller's money, or a loan from Aunt Sally. It could also be a credit line, a private investor, hard money lender or anyone else for that matter. It is very important to understand this concept.

Now, if you were to purchase a house and put down 20% which you borrowed from your relative, then you would have purchased the house with no money down. You can call it 100% financing or whatever you want. As far as the bank is concerned you put down 20%. However there is a problem with that, since as many mortgage brokers will tell you that banks want to know the source of the funds. When they see that the funds are borrowed and that you have no "skin" (your own money) in the deal, then they will reject the loan.

So, what is an investor with no cash going to do to get around this problem? The solution is to borrow ALL of the money to purchase the house for cash. If you borrow all of the cash from Uncle Bob, then you can be a cash buyer. Cash buyers are very rare today and if you are a cash buyer then you can buy bank-owned REO properties at a substantial discount to market value.

However, Uncle Bob is not going to feel comfortable loaning you money to buy a house unless there is substantial security for him. Since banks loan money at loan to value (LTV) ratios of 70%, Uncle Bob might be especially cautious and only agree to loan money at 60% LTV. Is this risky for him? Well it is less risky than conventional mortgages that are funded by banks. Why is it less risky? Conventional banks lend based on a mortgage application, a credit score and an appraisal. But Uncle Bob is a little smarter than the average bank. He actually can go out to the property and inspect it himself. After all, if you don't pay him he is going to get the property, since he has the first mortgage.

So Uncle Bob is going to need to have enough

knowledge of real estate to feel comfortable that, if you don't pay him and he gets your house, that he will have a deal. Uncle Bob is going to do his own computations and he is not going to rely on an appraiser. Uncle Bob is going to spend days or even weeks investigating the property, compared to the 30 minutes that an out-of-state loan officer looks at a file. If Uncle Bob is convinced that your deal is a good deal, then he is going to loan the money. If you are paying him 10% interest and the bank is only paying him 2% then Uncle Bob will make more money loaning on real estate compared to having his money in the bank. If Uncle Bob has done his homework then he will only fund a deal at 60% LTV or less; if he thinks the house is worth $100,000, he will only loan you $60,000 and no more.

Your challenge will be to find a $100,000 house that you can buy for $60,000. Being a cash buyer will make your job much easier, because 99% of the buyers that are competing with you will be looking to get a mortgage. Currently it is very difficult to get anything other than an FHA or VA loan. Cash buyers are able to buy properties directly from banks for as little as 50 cents on the dollar. This is a once-in–a-lifetime opportunity.

So start looking for "Uncle Bob" or anyone that you know that has money. Then once you have an investor lined up, begin looking for wholesale real estate deals. When you find a deal, the mechanics will work like this:

House is worth	$100,000
You purchase for	$ 60,000
Uncle Bob loans	$ 60,000
Money out of pocket	$ 0

Now that you own the house, you will wait 6 to 12 months for something called "seasoning of the title" and then go to your mortgage broker and tell him that you want to do a refinance. You want to get a conventional mortgage at 7% to pay off Uncle Bob at 10%. The bank will require an appraisal and, if you were correct in your initial assessments, the appraisal should come in at $100,000. If the bank agrees to give you an LTV loan for 70% of the $100,000 appraisal, then they will loan you $70,000. Assume closing costs are $5,000, so after paying Uncle Bob back the $60,000 you are left with the following scenario:

House value	$100,000
Bank Loan	$ 70,000
Equity	$ 30,000
Cash left over from refinance	$ 5,000

You just purchased a house with no money down, and you now have $5,000 in your pocket and $30,000 of equity in the house. This is called distressed real estate investing. Your challenge is not finding Uncle Bob - there are many Uncle Bobs out there. They are called hard money lenders or private investors. Your challenge is to find a $100,000 house that you can buy for $60,000. That is the hard part. To do this you are going to need to find a distressed seller. If you can learn how to do that then you will have no problem finding the money.

Beginner distressed real estate investors think that finding the money and having good credit are the obstacles to their beginning to invest in real estate. This is not true. The biggest obstacle is education. Learn and understand how and why you can buy a $100,000 house for $60,000. Understand and know what a distressed seller is and why they would sell a house for less than its current value. Then go out and start looking for a deal.

6. Buying Foreclosed Properties.

Some of the greatest returns on real estate investments are earned by purchasing foreclosed or distressed properties for a fraction of the price. By investing money in foreclosed properties, savvy real estate investors have learned that they can purchase real estate property significantly under value. You can do it too if you do your research and avoid common pitfalls.

With every type of investment, there is risk. In most cases the higher the amount of risk that you are willing to take, the larger the returns on your investment. The same is true in real estate investing. This means that the properties that stand to make you the most money also present the most challenges.

While there are three stages of the foreclosure process where it is possible to purchase a distressed property, only one offers the greatest return. This is the Sheriff's sale or auction phase. If you are able to purchase a property at this time, you could realistically take ownership of the property for as much as 45 percent under the listing price of the home. But with this reward comes great risk.

The greatest way to minimize risk when investing in real estate is to do your homework. Here's a checklist to help you out:

• Find out how much of a cash deposit you will need at auction. In many cases, this is 10%, with the remaining balance due within months, weeks, days, or hours. Make sure that you know the laws in your state and county.

• Try your best to inspect the property before the auction. If you cannot inspect the property, strive to build up a relationship with the homeowner so that you can learn about any costly repairs that need to be done and calculate them into your bid price. Verify that there are no other liens on the property through a title search. If you purchase the property at auction, these will become your responsibility.

• Know your competition. Since the original lender for the property wins at auction 80% of the time, forming a relationship with the lender is a good idea.

• Set a bid price and stick with it. Avoid becoming emotionally involved in the bidding process, which can lead to over-bidding. Have a solid idea of what you are investing in, how much you are willing to pay for it, and what type of return you expect.

• Remember; the goal of investing is to minimize risk and maximize profit. By doing your homework before the auction, you will be sure to do both. Never buy a property blindly. Doing so only sets you up for failures that will cut into your profit margin.

Would you buy homes if you could get them for 31 cents on the dollar? I mean, would you pay $62,000 for a home worth $200,000? I know that sounds crazy, but I also know it's happening right now, today!

"Fortunes are made when blood is in the streets." You've heard that one, right. Well, when it comes to the housing crisis in the U.S., blood is in the streets and fortunes are not being made, but augmented. It's the folks who already have fortunes that are buying American real estate at "dollar store" prices. I'm talking about sovereign wealth funds.

Let me remind you exactly what a sovereign wealth fund (SWF) is. A SWF is a state-owned investment fund composed of financial assets and pools of money derived from a country's reserves, which are set aside for investment purposes that will benefit the country's economy and citizens. The funding for a

SWF comes from central bank reserves that accumulate as a result of budget and trade surpluses, and even from revenue generated from the exports of natural resources.

It boils down to this: The U.S. has been buying way more from other countries then they have been buying from us. We have all that stuff that we purchased through Wal-Mart, and they have all our money. In our modern world, all that wealth is really just a few digital computer blips. If it were actual thousand dollar bills they would have enough to overflow China's Bird Nest Stadium! We are experiencing the greatest transfer of wealth the world has ever seen. For those of us in the U.S., the wealth is traveling in the wrong direction. The amount of money in these funds is mind-boggling. As of May 2007, the United Arab Emirate's fund alone was worth more than $875 billion.

The estimated value of all SWF cash is estimated to be $2.5 trillion and growing. Due to the Washington politicians' self-serving fiscal policies, the value of the dollar has been dropping faster then a lead balloon. No one with the slightest understanding of economics wants to own something that continues to drop in value, and that includes managers of the sovereign wealth funds. The SWFs are using our dollars to buy up assets with appreciating value around the world. In the U.S., this includes valuable real estate like the Chrysler Building, which was purchased by an Abu Dhabi fund.

But here's the big news. The funds are now ready to grab tens of thousands of foreclosed homes in the U.S. When a bank takes back a home it goes into their REO account. REO stand for real estate owned, and banks have thousands and thousands of owned homes sitting vacant. They have far more homes available then interested buyers... until now. The SWFs are turning those depreciating Wal-Mart dollars into solid real estate assets. The sovereign wealth funds are operated by smart guys and they can recognize opportunity when they see it. American bankers are desperate, and the SWFs have big money. Do you think some sweet deals are going down? You bet your FICO score they are. These are cash deals that may save some banks from going under.

One buyer representing a SWF is now willing to pay 50 cents to 60 cents on the dollar for a collection of California REOs worth, at a minimum, $500 million. It is reported that this same buyer negotiated a $2 billion package mixed with homes across the country for 31 cents on the dollar.

Here's where you should ask, "So what? Why should I care?" Well, those funds must profit from their investment by offering those homes for sale. Since they purchased them at deep discounts they can sell them at discount prices. When you under-cut market prices, you bring down the value of all homes in the market. That means an increased number of people will find they owe more on their mortgage then their home is worth. That could potentially mean more foreclosures, more homes offered at discount prices and a further drop in value for all homes.

Real estate investment is a critical decision, to be taken only with detailed knowledge of the industry to predict the future profit. Foreclosure investing is one of the biggest and the most significant investments of one's lifetime. So before you make the decision, the first thing you should do is to understand the detailed and subtle components and methods of real estate foreclosure investing.

Every loan comes up with specific repayment terms and conditions. The initial rules focus on the interest rate and the tenure period. If a borrower fails to pay off the loan amount in time, then the lender pre-claims the property by turning off the loan. The property then goes to foreclosure sale. If you have a plan to buy real estate, then it is always wise to go for real estate foreclosure investing, because here the percentage of the return on investment is high.

The foreclosed properties are sold under the supervision of courts or a selected trustee. The first case is known as Judicial Foreclosure, while the second one is the Statutory Foreclosure. But if you want to fetch the highest profit from this real estate foreclosure investing, then you must play a significant role throughout the foreclosure process.

Your work in real estate foreclosure investing may start at the very initial stage, when a borrower receives a summons from his or her lender. To know this, you have to practice high-level networking and determine a reliable source for your regular updates. At this stage, you have to choose the right property and make the preliminary property investigation so you can make the right investment decision.

The next stage of a foreclosure makes a public record of the pending legal action. To act judiciously, you have to identify the other intended investors and estimate their investment capacity. You have to start the negotiation process from this very stage, because you have a limited time to negotiate with the owners and the lenders.

If the owner fails to pay off the loan even at this last stage, then the property goes up for sale. Generally, the bid amount covers the amount owed to the lender. If the sale value rises, the lender gains the profit. Even at this last stage of real estate foreclosure investing, you have to be very cautious in dealing with the lenders and making your bids. If anyhow the property misses to fetch a proper amount, then it becomes a REO (real estate owned).

7. Buying Parking Spaces.

One of the more unusual but sometimes profitable real estate investments is buying parking spaces. In every large city, including Chicago, there is always a need for parking, and demand outpaces supply. Even with public transportation readily available in large cities, the high gas prices, and the growing trend of green living and conservation, Americans still love their automobiles. Parking spaces are always going to be needed, and there are investors who are banking on it.

For example, in Chicago, the mayor had proposed lowering the number of unpaid parking tickets from three to two before you get booted. Right now it costs $60 to get a booted car back, along with paying all tickets owed. A booted car will be towed after 24 hours, so you could have an additional towing fee of about $150 plus storage costs. It could add up to several hundred dollars in a few days. Records show that there were almost 59,000 cars booted in Chicago in 2007, so this city obviously has a need for parking that isn't being met.

How much does a deeded parking space cost? It depends on where you are located. In New York, it's possible to pay more than $175,000 for a prime parking spot. In Chicago, deeded parking spaces run anywhere from $20,000 to $65,000, or more in some of the trendy new construction high-rises or downtown locations. High profile developments like the Chicago Spire usually allow for parking for all of its future residents for a fee in addition to the condo price. Some buyers will opt for a second space if one is available, and others may decide not to purchase one at all. In many smaller Chicago real estate developments, no parking is offered with the condos.

According to Parkingsearch, the value of parking spaces has increased by quite a bit over the past few years. Their research finds that in Chicago, the average parking space sold for $28,000. By 2006 that increased to $30,000, and in 2007 it was about $33,000. With a fixed rate loan of 6% there is definitely a profit to be made. It may be a bit if a challenge to find a bank to loan you the money, but it is certainly doable. Your monthly payment should be in the range of $200, and the going rate for renting a parking space in prime spots can be as much as $300 to $500.

You need to keep in mind that you'll have a few fees associated with owning a parking space. It isn't all profit. While you won't have much upkeep on the spot, you will probably have to pay a maintenance fee to the building or condo association. A deed must be obtained, liability insurance is a good idea, and yearly taxes must be paid.

When looking for a good parking space investment, factors such as the garage being heated, secure entrances, and the level or floor in a multi-level garage all come into play. Having an elevator can increase the value. You should also do your research and see how well the units in the building have sold. Buying a parking space in a building that is only half sold or rented won't be a good investment.

Some real estate agents may be able to help you find available parking spaces, and many developers are turning to auction houses to liquidate condo inventory, including parking spaces, at a deep discount. Around 27 spaces at Millennium Center were auctioned off last spring, and 10 of those were sold absolute. The suggested opening bid for those spaces was $10,000 to $12,000, and they had been priced at $49,000 to $65,000 each. Parking spaces as investments may have never occurred to you, but next time you get a parking ticket or find your car booted, it may sound like a fantastic idea.

As you can see, getting into the real estate game and making money is possible, regardless of whether or not you have impeccable credit or a mountain of cash at your disposal. I've identified just seven ways that you can get involved in real estate investing on a scale congruent to your level of experience and your willingness to take on risk. There are many others that you can learn. A good real estate coach can provide advice and insider knowledge about these and many other, more advanced real estate investing techniques. Regardless of whether you seek out a mentor or fly solo, real estate investing provides you with multiple ways of creating wealth and a much brighter future. You won't get rich overnight, but by being smart and learning the ropes, real estate investing can be your ticket to a secure future.

25

How To Invest In Art

Collecting fine art is quickly becoming a more common method of investing and saving money. Putting your money into works of art can result in more of a return than a regular savings account, which is contrary to what most people believe. Many people don't think of fine art collecting when it comes to managing their money - but nothing could be further from the truth. Here are some common myths about fine art investments and investment.

One of the biggest myths concerning fine art collecting is that it doesn't appreciate quickly enough to be a good investment. Other widely-held but false assumptions tell you that art doesn't do well in a down-turning economy and that prints aren't valuable. This chapter should dispel each of those myths and prove that art can be a suitable way to improve your investment portfolio.

MYTH: Art doesn't appreciate as fast as traditional investments.

TRUTH: This couldn't be further from the truth. A piece by Andy Warhol worth $1,000 in 2005 is worth about $3,250 today. Simply put, the art market is consistently showing impressive returns, often beating out traditional investments. Two business professors from New York University agree. Michael Moses and Jiang-ping Mei have complied and tracked the performance of fine art. The Mei Moses Index covers Impressionist, Modern, American (before 1950), and Old Master artists. "From last year, through the end of 2007, all our index was up 20% while the S&P total return was up 5%," says Michael Moses, co-founder of Beautiful Asset Advisors.

MYTH: Art investments don't do well in a down-turning economy.

TRUTH: Fine art collecting is known to be a recession-proof method of investing. Because art values aren't dependent on any country's stock market or currency, they can continue to appreciate over time, regardless of the current state of the economy. For example, foreclosures have crippled the real estate market, but fine art investments continue to do well. Well-known artists like Marc Chagall, Pablo Picasso, and Andy Warhol are some of the many whose works continue to appreciate in value. The reason for this is simple: these artists are no longer living, limiting the number of original pieces available for sale.

MYTH: Prints aren't valuable.

TRUTH: An original, authentic, limited edition fine art print created during the artist's lifetime carries with it the value of being printed by the artist's hand. That is impossible to reproduce, and that is why it will always be valuable.

When most people think of prints, they think of mass-produced posters that can be found anywhere. In the art world, a print has a completely different definition. An art print is usually produced in limited editions that are often hand-signed by the artist. Usually you can find a number such as 15/150 which means that your copy was the 15th of a total edition of 150 (frequently there are also a few artist proofs). These collectible works were printed under the artist's direction and with the artist's approval. The plates used to make the prints were almost always destroyed shortly after the print run. This means that the prints are in limited supply and it impossible to recreate an original.

Art has proven to be a unique investment opportunity that is sure to appreciate while you enjoy its beauty every day. With the Internet making it easier than ever to source artworks, it is also relatively simple these days to build up a great-looking collection.

While prices for unique works are increasingly beyond the reach of many, limited editions of, say, 150 plus are financially and widely accessible, making it possible to acquire pieces by major artists for reasonable prices. There can be a downside, however. While little beats the pleasure that a signed work can bring, generally speaking, the larger an edition, the less likely it is to appreciate in value quickly - or even substantially.

Nevertheless, the contemporary art market is full of contradictions and, with growing demand at all levels, recent trends have often seen this assumption overturned.

As an obvious example, Damien Hirst's early prints for Eyestorm consistently fetch $10,000-$16,000 at re-sale, a very substantial profit on their original price. More recently, prints by Banksy and other urban artists have proved equally lucrative.

In other words, it's becoming increasingly possible - although by no means a certainty - to make substantial profits quickly with relatively little outlay, although the trick, as always, is knowing what to buy and when to sell.

The art world has a curious attitude to speculation. Buying and selling purely for profit is still regarded as just a little unsavoury, even though the entire art market is dedicated to this pursuit. Perhaps it's because art has such a curiously dual nature, combining aesthetic and cultural worth with a commercial value that can reach very high sums indeed.

Whatever the case, it would be difficult to consistently make money from art without some genuine appreciation and an insight into what will stand the test of time. Many dealers are themselves collectors, at least partly funding their own acquisitions through trading. Yet it's certainly true that with contemporary art consistently showing remarkable returns on investment, it's also become an attractive proposition to a very wide range of buyers.

In general, non-specialist speculators often trade in the work of artists whose frequent media coverage makes them well-known to the public. As shown by the two examples mentioned above, this can certainly reap substantial rewards. But it's also important to remember that in an increasingly novelty-driven world, the next big thing is usually just around the corner. Celebrity artists often take on the nature of a trend, and fads can become outdated with dramatic speed. Knowing when to sell such works is vitally important.

Ups and downs in the market aren't just related to artists with familiar public profiles, of course. The art world itself frequently generates its own, 'flavor of the month' buzz. A few years ago, Martin Kippenberger's prices rose dramatically, then leveled off just as quickly. Chinese and now Indian contemporary art have been subject to the same kind of intensely fashion-led market trends. Clearly, money can be made by quickly identifying and speculating on trends, but you'll need to have your finger firmly on the pulse. Knowing what's considered exciting is essential, but you'll also have to determine how long this excitement is actually going to last.

When it comes to collecting art, you'll often read the following: the safest way to build a collection is simply to buy work you really like. Such advice seems tailor-made to shield less knowledgeable collectors from potential disappointment, and perhaps even encourage sales of less desirable work. Buy a piece you love and if its value falls, no harm has been done. If it gains in price, that's a bonus. Of course it's important to purchase work you want to own and view. But since contemporary art presents real investment opportunities, it makes sense to think carefully about what to add to your collection. After all, look at almost any on-line art site, and you'll see that prices for fairly standard pieces are often equivalent to what you'd pay for work with far greater investment potential.

Although there's obviously no way of predicting definite future value, the key is to familiarize yourself as much as possible with the background of artists you're drawn to. How long have they been working? Is there a theme or thought process behind their work? Has this evolved coherently over the years? Artists with at least some degree of complexity and persistent 'vision' are generally more likely to gain steadily in appreciation and price. You'll also want to know if the artist has achieved some kind of recognition. Is their work held by collections, galleries or museums? Has it been exhibited consistently?

Professional opinion is yet another important factor in trying to determine an artist's long-term prospects. If a large number of critics and academics agree on their high opinion of an artist, this is another good sign that they will retain or even gain value.

Mid-career artists can be judged much more easily in relation to their existing work. After all, good art isn't just about something that happens to look nice on a wall. It's about a certain kind of commitment and an obvious path of development. If all these factors are present, buying probably makes sense. Limited editions by Jeff Koons, for example, were relatively inexpensive 5 or 6 years ago, but with recent record-breaking prices for major works, they have shot up in value.

Even artists who disappear temporarily from the art market radar are much more likely to re-emerge at a later point if they show the 'right' kind of commitment and passion. New young artists are often fizzing with ideas, many of which can seem ground-breaking or even radical, but the problem is that they have yet to prove their long-term worth.

That said, you can certainly gain an insight into their potential by applying the criteria above. It's especially important to determine if they have something genuine to express or are simply employing methods that could, over time, be seen as just a gimmick.

Of course, if you're looking to make a high return on investment, rapidly emerging artists can prove to be highly lucrative. In such cases, it's probably a good idea to invest in as substantial a piece as possible, although, as we've seen, editions and multiples can also prove money-earners. Keep a close eye on auction prices and signs of market fatigue. Such artists might be the talk of the town right now, but will they fulfill their early promise?

If, after a few years, their work appears stuck in a rut and prices seem to be leveling off or even dropping, it's time to think twice about their long-term appeal. On the other hand, if they do continue to create great work, any pieces bought for relatively low sums at the start of their careers should steadily rise in value.

If you're lucky enough to have substantial sums of money to spend on art, newer artists, as we have seen, can produce significant return on investment. But perhaps the best way to offset the risks that they may never fulfill expectations is to 'spread your bets' across a selection of up and coming names. Buying the work of several different artists might mean settling for less significant works, but with the right kind of knowledge - and luck - hitting a jackpot is still possible.

If you've done your research, the chances are fairly good that at least one - and hopefully more - of your chosen artists will gain in recognition. And, given the phenomenal increase in prices for contemporary art, if that happens, eventual profits could far outweigh the costs of initial purchases, even if other works fail to make the grade.

It's worth remembering that many well-known collectors buy huge amounts of work by new, 'promising' artists. Charles Saatchi is a particularly good example, and although he is famous for the apparent strength of his collection, a sizeable proportion of the artists he has collected over the years have faded into obscurity (you won't see these listed on his website!). However, the phenomenal rise in value of those who went on to become major names - Peter Doig, for example - have reaped him many millions of dollars in overall profit. And if those are the rewards, you can probably afford to make the odd mistake.

26

How To Invest In
Gems and Jewelry

The value of gems have proven to increase over time. They also are sometimes preferred because they are tangible assets compared to bonds and stock: you can actually wear them! It is generally expected that gem stones will increase in value over the next decades as they are slowly getting harder to find and the demand is rising. They are also protected against inflation, unlike money or stock. Gems are secure investments if you know how to choose the rights ones to invest in.

The key to investing in gems is to start slow and build your way up. You don't need to be rich to start: $1500 can get you started in no time. Finding a good gem dealer is crucial in making your investment profitable. Get to know them and check their references and lab certificates. Ask for money back guarantees. When you have found a good gem dealer, choose your gems carefully depending on color and size. Then keep your investment for a while, at least 5-10 years. That is the best way to make a profit.

To the serious and single-minded investor, gold, platinum and silver jewelry items are unlikely to come near the top of the list of potentially profitable opportunities that he or she will research. It is reasonable to propose that before venturing into this market a tremendous amount of investigation should be carried out and knowledge assimilated that is not relevant to other investment vehicle.

Reliable contacts and dealers in the jewelry trade must be sought out and cultivated. Perhaps most importantly, the investor should treat jewelry as an all-consuming hobby, so that collecting aesthetically pleasing items that may or may not show a profit will still give pleasure. This is as good a reason as any to explain why many savvy female investors take an interest in this market.

Silver jewelry as an investment, unless in the specialized antique market, is unlikely to provide serious investment opportunities unless sufficient volume can be purchased to produce a profit on the meltdown value of the metal.

Antique jewelry, with or without gemstones, follows the pattern of other antique items in that age is not the overriding factor. There will be items 100 years old or more that may not have sufficient scarcity value to attract buyers into paying a premium over the basic value of the metal and gemstone content. Entering this end of the market will therefore require an additional specialized knowledge of antiques and hallmarks.

Gold jewelry has been around for thousands of years; it has never gone out of fashion, and never dates or fades. As a consequence, there is a choice of two investment paths to take - antique or modern.

Gold has a tendency to wear away over time and decrease in volume and weight when in use. It can also be subject to scratching, resulting in loss of weight. It is important to be familiar with the hallmarks and the symbols denoting purity. 18K means that the item is 75% pure, 14K = 58.5% pure. 1K is one twenty fourth part of 100% pure metal.

The balance is made up of other ingredients to make the item more durable or whiter. It is believed that half of all the gold sold in the United States is stamped with a false Karat weighting, so only deal with established, reliable and registered merchants.

Trust is paramount; it is easy for jewelers to take advantage of unsuspecting investors who are not fully versed in the pitfalls of the market.

Unlike gold, platinum does not have a long history of use in jewelry; anything earlier than 1900 is rare indeed. Examples of Edwardian platinum jewelry - often rings set with gemstones - can be purchased, but beware of modern antique-style platinum jewelry. Studying antique platinum jewelry will need less application than studying gold, but it is essential to have a sound knowledge, particularly of the hallmarks, before entering the market. Platinum is over thirty times rarer than gold. Most of the platinum used in jewelry is between 90% and 95 % pure. The content is indicated in parts per thousand rather than Karats.

The properties of platinum allow for more intricate and finer jewelry designs than possible with gold. Platinum is considerably more durable than gold and will wear better and last longer in use. Platinum is more resistant to scratching than gold and, if this occurs, the metal is displaced and can be restored by a specialist. Platinum jewelry has become extremely fashionable and could be considered as the preferred jewelry of choice amongst the affluent.

In the United States during World War Two, platinum was designated as a strategic metal and supplies were cut off from the jewelry trade. Items that can be guaranteed as sourced from this period will have a considerable rarity value. As with gold, find a trusted and established dealer before parting with your money.

Bear in mind that the current value of the metal content of the piece and a view on the future direction of the price of the metal become intrinsic factors in determining its potential as an investment. The Koh-I-Nor diamond is probably the best known of all gems. It is found in the British Crown Jewels collection, set in platinum. Many will say that you get more for your money when investing in platinum.

Palladium, which is recognized as a Platinum Group Metal (PGM), has overtaken platinum in its use in jewelry manufacture. Both metals have considerable use in industry, particularly in automobile manufacturing where they are often interchangeable, so that usage depends on the price/supply differences. When one has a price or supply advantage over the other, a buying opportunity may occur in the jewelry market, opening opportunities for you.

Investing in precious metal jewelry means entering a highly specialized market with many hazards for the unwary and ill-equipped. Trust and integrity are priorities when buying or selling through a dealer in the market place. There is no substitute for intensive research into all aspects, not only the jewelry application, of the metal under consideration as an investment. As an investment guru once said, "If in doubt, stay out."

However, you can invest in gems and jewelry for a fraction of the cost. The first secret is aligning yourself with the companies that handle the sales of estates and homes of the deceased. You can create relationships with the owners of these companies and ask if you can inspect all the jewelry (whether costume or fine) prior to the estate sale dates. In exchange, you can help publicize their upcoming sale by notifying antique dealers, shop owners and specialty store retailers who may be in the market for great furniture, rugs and accessories.

To the estate disposal companies, this help is

invaluable, as it raises their chances of getting better than fair market value when they sell to resellers. There is a second part to this secret, which also works with auctioneers who do general auctions of household and personal items. Once you have developed these relationships, they will call you prior to an auction and may agree to sell to you before the auction preview at a low box-lot price.

The second secret is to align yourself with pawn-shop owners. They do not sell costume jewelry, which to them has really no intrinsic value, but will offer a bulk price for costume jewelry brought in, and sell it to you for a small profit. You can acquire the most amazing pieces this way. A person who has unfortunately hit a rough spot and needs cash will usually clean out all of his drawers, which may include a lot of fine but most likely more costume jewelry. The pawn-broker knows he has an instant sale of any and all costume jewelry, and he will most likely sell it to you as a boxed lot. The person needing the money wins, the pawnbroker wins and you really win, because many of the items may have been in the family for years and may date back to the late 1930s or earlier. Some may be trash, but there are always at least one or two pieces that make the transaction a success.

The third secret, and one that takes tact and sensitivity, is when a widower or children of a recently deceased family member is trying to move on and feels the need to donate or "clean out" their belongings and personal effects. By advertising in the local newspaper or "pennysaver magazine" stating that you pay cash for any costume jewelry, you can encourage such people to call you. You should always give them a more than fair price for the items they have, and you will acquire more wonderful treasures to add to your collection. After a few years of using the above secrets, people will come to know you as the jewelry man or lady and the calls will consistently come in, and the jewelry selections will continue to improve.

If you are thinking of making money by selling gold jewelry, start by taking it to a local pawnshop to see what you are offered. Pawnshops generally weigh your gold and will offer you a price based upon the current wholesale value of the precious metal. This will probably be much lower than the item is worth as jewelry, but it gives you immediate access to cash that may be worthwhile in the case of broken or damaged jewelry.

Next, find out how much local jewelry stores will offer to pay you for your gold jewelry. Sometimes they will only offer to sell the item on consignment, which means that you leave the jewelry in their store, and if it gets sold they will collect a commission. Other times, if they feel that the item has a good resale value, they will offer to buy your gold jewelry outright. It all depends on the preference of the particular store, so be prepared to visit more than one.

Another option is to take out a classified ad in the local newspaper. Advertising in newspaper classifieds, especially in the Sunday edition of the newspaper, is an excellent way to let local people know that you have gold jewelry for sale. You should, however, exercise common sense in how you approach dealing with the public.

Alternatively, you could sell your gold jewelry to a local precious metals merchant. Although such businesses routinely deal with gold coins and bullion, they are often quite happy to take gold jewelry. As long as it is gold, they will make you a fair offer. The problem is that the offer will be based upon the current melt value of the gold, so it may be best to reserve this option places for broken or damaged jewelry that cannot be sold anywhere else.

If you can't get a good price for your gold jewelry locally, then try to sell your gold jewelry on-line at eBay or another auction website. The best deal for your gold jewelry may come from someone in a completely different part of the country, so you may as well put your gold on the auction block to see how much people are willing to pay.

27

How To Invest In Collectible Cars

Your antique cars may look very old and seem to be of no value. But there is a way to make money from most of them. For many old cars, a little restoration may be enough to easily sell them to people who like collecting antique cars.

The value of any antique item can be increased if you provide it with a new look and restore life to it. Let me give you some advice on how to make your antique cars profitable by restoring and selling them.

1. Look for enough space.

The first step for restoring your old cars is looking for enough space to do the job. This will depend on how many antique cars you are going to repair. Furthermore, take into consideration the room needed when dismantling the parts of each car and building up the car again.

2. Use original parts as much as possible.

This helps to increase the value of your car and convince your prospective buyer that your asking price is justified.

3. Give your car a new look through research.

If you do not have enough knowledge on the specific car you are restoring, you can read car magazines or search the Internet to educate yourself on how to enhance the look and performance of your car. You can be creative, but make sure that your antique cars will have the original look that it had when it first came out on the market.

4. Seek the help of a professional.

This is recommended if you have exhausted all your knowledge, time, expertise and money when restoring antique cars. There may be situations in which seeking a professional help would be better than doing the job yourself.

Selling the Car:

1. Maintain the car.
Once you are done with the restoration process, your car is now ready to be sold. Since the process may take some time, ensure that your car is clean and working properly at all times.

2. Set the car's market value.
Have a detailed list of the prices of your cars should a buyer be interested in understanding your costing.

3. Know your cars.
It is important that you know the product you are selling. Some buyers are not knowledgeable enough about the cars they are looking to purchase. They may ask questions such as history of the vehicle, manufacturer, how to maintain the car and even if you have a copy of its manual; it is better that you are prepared to answer any question that a buyer may have so you can easily convince them to accept your asking price.

4. Advertise when possible.

There are a lot of free classified ads where you can advertise your antique cars. Additionally, you can also post a message about your antique cars on boards regarding automobiles (if you are allowed). Look for free or cheap venues to market your product.

Antique cars can be profitable if you properly invest your money, time, knowledge, creativity and patience. Moreover, it will serve as an achievement once you gave life to the old and rusted metals. If you pay any attention to the major collector car auctions held every year, you probably think you cannot afford a collector car anymore. The prices seem to have shot through the roof to the point of being ridiculous.

Let me assure you that unless you are looking for a museum piece that you would not want to drive on any road today, there is clearly hope. Many people have bought and sold collector cars and trucks over the years.

In the last couple of days I found some examples of great buys that collectors would be pleased to own. These cars are not showroom pieces, but who cares? They are nice rides that you and I could enjoy for a fraction of the cost of other cars. Take this 1971 Chevy El Camino, found on *Craigs List* (www.CraigsList.org). The car has a 350 V8 engine with a Turbo 350 automatic transmission, power steering, power disc brakes, and custom wheels. They are asking $2800 OBO. (OBO means "or best offer".)

Any time someone advertises OBO, you know they will take less. This is your opportunity to buy for a fraction of the cost. It is up to your negotiation skills to determine just how much less they will take. Now this has a lot to do with just where the seller is at in their efforts to sell. If you catch them when they really want to unload the burden they have of owning that vehicle (for all kinds of reasons), you can usually get a substantial savings when you buy.

Another example is a 1970 Mustang Coupe, also found on *Craig's List*. It shows a straight no-rust body, has a 302 V8 engine, automatic transmission, power steering, power brakes, and chrome wheels. They are asking $2200 OBO and you should not expect to get too much off on this one, for it is pretty cheap already.

These are just a couple of examples of what might interest you. You can buy a collector car today for a reasonable cost, and you can find an incredible variety of collector cars and trucks like these advertized almost every day. These may not be your preference, but there are many more where these came from. Keep in mind that these are very low cost vehicles that would get you into the collector car arena. There is almost an exponential increase in the number of cars you can buy with every $500 you add to your buying power.

There are several factors that may affect the car's value. One of these is the auction price. In an auction, the price is usually set at the lowest possible bid and then people are asked to raise the bid. The highest bidder gets the item that is up for auction. An antique car price guide may state the lowest possible price for a certain car. Of course, the price of the car in the antique car price guide could differ vastly from a specific car due to other factors. The antique car price guide is just a guide, not a direct price list.

Another factor that can affect the value of an antique automobile is its asking price. Asking prices are based on the amount of money and effort spent on the restoration of the car. This does not necessarily mean that this is the selling price. The antique car price guide can guide you on the range of a specific car's prices. The range allows for shoddy restoration and professional restoration, which can be the minimum and maximum prices.

Celebrity ownership may also alter the actual price of the car from the antique car price guide. If a certain car was previously owned by a well-known celebrity or royalty, its price is probably going to be higher than other cars of the same make and model. Of course, if the car is in bad shape, then no matter which celebrity owned it, the price will belong to the lower price range indicate in the antique car price guide.

The originality of the car can also boost its price. The antique car price guide may set a maximum price for a specific car model and make, but this usually is base on restored cars. Antique cars that have little restoration done to them, or which have most of their original parts intact and functional, tend to have higher prices than other restored cars of the same make and model.

Classic cars have a different set of investment criteria. It is easier to spot a classic car than to know how much it is worth. You may know that the Oldsmobile Cutlass sitting in your garage is a real sweet vintage ride, but you might have a difficult time deciding how much to sell it. Or maybe you have spotted that Cutlass, but do not know whether the price is worth it.

Worry no more, as here is an easy guide on how to estimate classic car values.

1. Research Market Values from Dealers

Classic car values are almost always fluctuating, as all car values are. By researching the market value of a classic car sold by professional dealers, you can have a clear marker as to how much a vehicle in a certain condition is worth. However, remember that this is a dealer's price, so expect that it is overpriced by between ten and twenty percent. There are many other determinants of price that are often not covered by dealer-based values, such as your own preference and the demand for that car. Nonetheless, market values from dealers are still a good marker.

2. Check the Condition of the Car

The condition of the car is usually the biggest determinant of its value. Most classic car enthusiasts use a five-point rating system, as follows:

• Excellent: A car in perfect and near-mint condition, usually drivable.
• Very Good: A car with some very minor scratches or engine and mechanism faults, but is still almost perfect and drivable.
• Good: A car with some very repairable damages, but still needs little effort to restore and is still drivable.
• Fair: A car that needs a lot of restoration work, with

signs of abuse such as dents, scratches, and rust. If a car is not drivable because of engine, brake, or other mechanical failures, but has a solid exterior look, it will fall in this category.

•Parts car: A car that cannot be plausibly restored because of heavy damage. A part car, as its name suggests, is usually bought only for its reusable parts.

A car in an excellent condition could be sold for twice or thrice its original price and collectors will still buy it. Cars in the good or fair condition are the usual ones that you will see in the market.

3. Customization is a Minus

A classic car with air conditioning, a fuel-efficient engine, and soft seats may be convenient, but these modifications often bring down the value of a car. Customized paint jobs may look cool, but they still decrease the possible price. The reason for this is simple: original parts are harder to find, and maintaining them are more difficult too. Expect a car with almost all original parts (including the wheels) and paint color to have a really high price tag attached to it.

4. Rarity is a Plus.

Classic Dodge Chargers may be valued highly, but a Charger with a Hemi engine is a gold mine. This is because Hemi engine-equipped Chargers were made in very limited numbers. If you have one in your old man's garage, you may want to reconsider that engine change. Look for the rare cars.

5. Original Options are a Plus.

Turbo and superchargers might increase a muscle car's values, given that they are original parts. Because the '61 Bullet T-Bird is used as a pace car for Indianapolis 500, it has some original era modifications which increase its value.

When buying or selling classic cars, remember to consider the condition, the originality, rarity, and the added options. Put this side by side with the market value from dealers, and adjust as needed.

28

Make Money with Stocks, Bonds, and Mutual Funds

When times are financially tough, some people love stocks while others stay far away from them. The stock market (Dow Jones) usually drops or wavers in an unstable manner when a recession hits, and that usually creates a fear of it. But in reality, if you know how to play the market right, this may be a good time to invest. That's because often you can buy cheap in a 'bear' market.

What does all this mean? Let's start at the beginning. A stock is a part of a company, a stake. When you buy a stock, it means that you have some level of ownership in the company. If the company does well, then you do well. If the company fails, well, then you won't be seeing your money again.

Most stock-holders have a stake in the company on paper. That means that they don't own enough stock to really have a voice in the day–to-day matters, but they may be invited to attend an annual stockholders meeting or company event. But each stock-holder has some ownership in the company and in the profits it makes.

Before you invest

The first rule in playing the stock market is to use your own money. Don't borrow money to invest; this is a great option for someone with some money put aside to potentially make more.

What the wealthy have known for years, and the non-wealthy have begun to understand in the past two decades, is that the stock market is a viable way to make money, if you invest wisely. Most Americans worked hard to earn money, laboring at a job to bring in money. The rich understood that their money could be doing the work, and they let their money bring in more money.

Whether you choose to invest your money in stocks, bonds or mutual funds, it is important that you understand where you are putting your money. I like to compare it to personal relationships that lead to marriage. In Western society, you meet and date someone before committing. You get to know more about them - the good and the bad. So, too, if you are going to enter into an investment "marriage", you should know everything about the product. Although it's definitely easier to part ways with your investment.

It's not enough to avoid investing in tips or rumors that you hear. You need to research before you invest. What does the company say about the investment? When a business is going to allow the public to purchase stocks, it must follow guidelines of the U.S. government that stipulates how much information it must make available. The company will issue a publication called a prospectus, which gives you a lot of information about the company's services or products, hoping to entice you to invest.

What do others say about the investment? Whether it is your college buddy who knows a lot about the stock market or your financial advisor, listen to what they are saying about the stock. It makes a difference if they recommend it (which usually means it is performing well) rather than if you come across it in an article you are reading. Beyond the current value of the stock, informed people will research it to determine if it is expected to increase in value or not. For example, if the company in question is about to under-go a major government tax audit, well, I'd recommend you stay away. Or if it's primary products are exported to a country that recently overthrew it's leader, maybe you should hold on a little longer before putting your money there.

And when you are ready to invest, generally the recommendation is to avoid buying shares on the initial offering. When a company first offers its stocks for sale, it is called the Initial Public Offering (IPO). Usually IPOs are held when large companies want to become publicly traded or when small or new companies need capital to grow. IPOs are risky investments and new traders are usually recommended to veer away from them. Because the company does not have a history of trading, it is impossible to predict how it will do once it goes public.

Earning money from stocks

When you invest in stocks, you can earn money in one of two ways:

1. Stock Values Go Up.

Let's say a stock is valued at $1 when you purchased it last week. If you purchased 10 shares, you paid $10 for them. That was last week. This week, there is a sense that the company is doing well. More people want to buy stocks in that company. They are willing to spend more. So the stock's value on the stock market goes up. Let's say it is now valued at $2 per share. The 10 shares you bought last week for $10 are now worth $20. That means you earned $10 just for sitting at home.

The idea is really to spend more in the stock market, so that if you invested $1000 last week, this week your stock could be valued at $2000. That's $1000 made just for sitting at home. Not a bad deal!

Realize, of course, that the stock is only worth money when you sell it. So while you are holding onto it, its value can increase...or it can go down too. You don't know what the actual worth of your stocks will be until you are ready to sell them.

2. Dividends.

Another way you can make money with stocks is through dividends. Dividends are more common in more established companies, those that have been around for a while. A dividend is a payment that shareholders receive based on the company's success, but regardless of the individual stock price. Usually distributed at the end of each financial quarter, this is a bonus that you can get for having invested in the company.

Stocks are most successful over the long-run. They are not designed to be an overnight money maker. If you have some money tucked aside that you don't need right now, a recession is a good time to watch the stock market and make a smart investment in a company you believe is 'underpriced' now but will perform well in the coming years

Most people have a hard time understanding the nuances of stocks, and will use a stock broker to represent them. A broker can help you build a portfolio, which is the collection of your investments, and manage the stocks on your behalf.

You probably don't realize this but there are thousands of stocks that you could invest in. Most people will invest in different stocks, and even in different types of stocks. Don't put all your money into one kind of stock – such as technology – in case that area doesn't do so well in the coming years. It is best to spread it around, to "diversify" as it is known in financial circles.

One way that stocks are categorized is by size. This is based on what investors believe that the entire company is worth – its market capitalization. A "small cap" is a company that has a market capitalization valued at a lower amount, "mid cap" would be a mid-size value, and "large cap" is a company with a market capitalization valued at billions of dollars. While the large cap companies are considered more stable to invest in, many stockholders prefer the small or medium cap companies which have greater risk and therefore greater returns.

Another way that stocks are categorized is by their growth rates. A company that grows quickly has a stock that grows quickly. If you get in early, when the growth is beginning, you can often get a great return on your investment. But at some point the growth will slow down, and then there is a declining interest in the stocks, which makes them less valuable. So know when to jump in and when to sell.

If you are planning to play the stock market, ask around to get recommendations for a good broker. And most important, talk to your accountant to make sure that your stocks are coordinated well with your taxes.

Protect your investments from capital gains taxes It's nice to invest your money and see a profit, but you want to make sure you don't get taxed down to the last dollar when you sell your stock. Unfortunately, the U.S. government seems to believe that everyone who invests in the stock market has money to burn. And of course, such "wealthy" people like yourself should pay high taxes. So it created tax laws that demanded that you pay the same taxes on stocks owned for less than a year than you do on your regular income. This could be as much as 40% in taxes on the profits of your stocks! And if you choose to hold on to your stocks, well, then this is now considered a long-term investment and you can be taxed up to 20% for them.

One recommended way to avoid unnecessary capital gains taxes, which is the tax issued on the profit you make – the difference between what you paid when you bought the stock and what you sold it for, is to put money into a Roth IRA. A Roth IRA is an Individual Retirement Account (named after Congressman William Roth), and it is designed for someone like yourself. Tax law allows individuals to put aside funds into the Roth IRA, and the interest earned is tax-free. It's a little more complicated than this, but your accountant or financial advisor can help you understand the benefits of putting some earnings into a Roth IRA.

Bonds

Earlier in the book we mentioned government bonds. Now let us discuss this in more detail. While some people believe that stocks offer a greater return on the dollar (if you choose the right stock), others will say that bonds have a greater comfort zone. In other words, there is greater security in investing in bonds.

What is a bond? In easy terms, it is a way for you to lend money to a company or to the government. You invest your money in the project or company, and you can earn interest on your loan. Usually you "buy a bond" (lend the money) for a specific period of time. When the loan is due back to you, it is referred to as the bond maturing. When the bond matures, you can cash it in and get your money back, or you can hold onto your bond and continue to earn interest on it.

While stocks are about buying ownership in something, bonds are about taking part in someone's debt. This may sound like a risky investment; but in the case of government bonds, it's advantageous, since debt holders are prioritized over shareholders when it comes to getting paid. Therefore, government bonds are a secure place to invest your money.

You can purchase bonds that have higher interest rates but have greater risk, or you can invest in U.S. government bonds, which often pay a lower rate of interest but are considered to be secure. In addition to government bonds (U.S. federal, municipal, or foreign government), other options for bond investment include corporate bonds and mortgage securities.

Bonds are often preferred over stocks, even though stocks can have greater returns. There are several advantages to bonds. First, some bonds are tax-free, which means you don't pay taxes on the interest you earn. Bonds are also good for the short-term; you usually don't have to keep them as long as stocks to see your profit. The two main reasons people prefer bonds over stocks is both for the regular income – giving you a better grasp of what your earnings will be and when - and because they are generally considered a safer investment that stocks. Bonds, on the whole, don't lose as much money as stocks.

Does that mean that bonds are a definite money-maker? In today's world, nothing is 100% certain. While bonds have a high level of security, there are still some risks involved. If you purchase a bond in a weak company, it may pay out a higher rate of interest but it is a riskier investment. These are called "junk bonds". And even if you invest in a safer bond, like a U.S. government bond, remember that the payment is fixed. If you hold the bond for a while, and inflation goes up, then the interest return to you may not be as high as the increasing costs of things you are buying.

Mutual Funds

If you are already exploring stocks and bonds, you should not overlook mutual funds. Studies have shown that the average interest rate on a savings account is less than two percent, while mutual funds produce an average annual return of ten percent. Mutual funds is also an easy way for you to diversify your funds (as most experts tell you to do) without having to take much time or effort to research everything.

What are mutual funds? Basically, they offer the opportunity for a lot of people just like you to invest money into a range of things. You would be joining thousands of people you don't know, to put your money into a whole range of investments, such as real estate, bonds, and specific stocks. The money is collectively invested, so if the mutual fund is successful, then you (and the thousands of other investors) earn money. If the mutual fund is not successful, then you (and the thousands of other investors) lose money.

A key advantage to participating in a mutual fund is that it can offer you an assortment of investments. Because you may not want to put all your money into one stock category, say high-tech, you can choose a mutual fund that invests in different areas. You also don't have to be that involved. If you want to invest in a mutual fund, there are companies that are designated for this financial investment, and they will monitor the portfolio and recommend to you whether to hold on to it or to sell it.

The fund manager's job is to be your eyes and ears, and this can help you tremendously if you are not a financial investment wizard or if you simply don't have the time to monitor your investment. When choosing a mutual fund, it is important to look into the track record of the fund and the experience of the fund manager in managing different funds.

When you have decided that mutual funds are the right investment for you, determine how much time you want to invest your money. You also have to think about how much risk you want. Funds that have been around for longer can show a performance history that may help you choose the place to invest. Or a good broker will do that as well.

There are two types of mutual funds. Load funds and No-Load funds. A no-load fund means that the mutual fund's shares are being sold without charging a sales fee or broker's commission. The investment company is selling shares directly. A load fund means that there is a charge, usually a commission that can be billed when the mutual fund is being bought or being sold

Many prefer a no-load mutual fund, believing that it is better for every dime invested to go towards the investment. This means if you invest $500, you will have bought $500 worth of mutual funds, and not directed anything towards a broker. In the past, people believed that a load fund was safer, as paying a commission meant that someone was doing homework, researching the best options for you. But research has shown that no-load funds are not necessarily weaker in performance than load funds.

29

On-Line Trading

Formerly, the stock market was a playing field for the wealthy. Until the 1990s, the affluent in America were significantly increasing their income, even doubling it, through the stock market. In fact, some say that many of the richest Americans used the stock market to reach the high rungs of affluence.

What changed in the 1990s is the role of on-line stock trading. Using the internet, smaller investors (in other words, those who are not rich) can be more active in the stock market. For those who want to earn more money in a hands-on effort, on-line investing can be an option, and even a career if you invest for others as well. While this is appealing because it can be done from any computer with internet connectivity and it doesn't require a lot of money, enter this arena with caution, though, as it is considered risky if you don't know your way around.

How do you start?

There are different kinds of on-line trading you can do, and you probably want to decide before you hire a broker, so that you can sign up with a firm that handles your kind of trading. You can choose between day trading, short-term trading, weekly trading or even monthly trading.

What makes day trading unique is that people rarely hold onto their shares past the close of market that day. Internet made this available to people like you and me. Until the growth of Internet, only major financial companies and banks had the access to the stock exchanges and the relevant market data to enable them to monitor and participate in daily trading. But technology has brought the information into our homes and private individuals like you and I can now be as informed as the great financial institutions.

Within day trading, there are different options too. For those who like the fast pace and have time, short term trading is an option. This is generally where you purchase stocks only to sell them literally within minutes. Some people try to protect themselves by trend trading, whereby they see a stock's price increasing and they jump along for the ride.

You can also choose how to invest your money. The Securities Exchange Commission has set limitations and restrictions on day trading with the U.S. stock market, but there are many opportunities to trade beyond that, including futures, options and currencies. Depending on your interest (or multiple interests), you must become familiar with the specific area. For example, if you want to trade currencies, you will learn about exchange rates (how does the U.S. dollar compare to the Euro or Japanese Yen, for example). Interested in commodities? Learn about oil, gold and wheat (or others).

Find a broker

To start trading on-line, it is recommended that you find a reliable brokerage firm. While you will be doing the trading and monitoring your portfolio, you need the information and technology from a company that has experience and credibility to start you off. In addition to a membership fee (which is usually under $50), you have to have a minimal amount of money on hand, usually around $500, to open an account.

A good broker can make all the difference in on-line trading. Not only should you confirm that the firm is legitimate (the Securities Exchange Commission of the U.S. government maintains a listing), but you should talk to clients of the firm and hear their experiences. Find a firm that handles new on-line traders well, and specifically the kind of trading you plan to do, so you can be sure that they will fully accommodate you and give you the attention you need.

The firm will provide you with information so that you can learn how to use their trading system, and you will have to invest in and learn how to use special software for on-line trading.

The next steps

With this information, you can access the stock market in "real" time and you will see how quickly things move. Don't invest until you are comfortable with the system. Review the history of the stocks you are thinking about investing in, and watch their performance for a little bit before you put your money into them.

Many brokerage houses that have on-line trading options have a huge amount of information available to clients so that you can learn how to increase your investments and profitability.

Managing your portfolio

When you are investing on-line, it's not just enough to buy shares with your money. You must learn how to manage your funds and portfolio if you want to be successful. Most experts will recommend that you maintain a diversified portfolio, investing in different types of stocks and different areas to provide greater protection for yourself.

There is a lot of information available on the Internet, and many free informational newsletters you can subscribe to, which can help you monitor trends, changing laws, and news about on-line trading. Arm yourself with as much information before you start, and keep yourself educated throughout your involvement in on-line trading.

30

Lending Money to the American Government

Y ou've heard mention of U.S. government bonds – what does that mean?

The American government needs a lot of money for its annual budget, and it also owes a lot of money, known as the federal debt. It uses money borrowed from citizens to finance itself, through Treasury bonds, Treasury notes and Treasury bills. If you play your cards right and invest wisely, you can be making money off the U.S. government!

Treasury Bonds and Notes are similar in the

concept, with the main difference being that Treasury Bonds usually need more than 5 years to mature while Treasury Notes generally mature between 1-5 years. Both Treasury Bonds and Notes are like regular corporate bonds, where you are loaning money and you receive interest on your investment. Generally, you receive interest payments once or twice a year, and then the full amount of the bond's worth upon maturity.

Treasury Bills are short term securities which enable you to invest money with the U.S. government for less than a year. Treasury Bills do not pay out interest; instead you can purchase them at a reduced rate from their face value, and then cash them in for their full value when they mature. For example, if one is valued at $500, you can purchase it at $450. At the end of the year, when it matures it pays out $500. Obviously, the more you invest, the more you can make with these Bills, and the payout is guaranteed

Advantage to Financing the U.S. Government

For those who have some money set aside but aren't ready to plunge into a risky venture like stocks, the U.S. savings bond is as secure as a bank but offers a better return on the money. With U.S. government bonds, like any bond, the longer you can commit the funds, the better the interest rate. Most people look to U.S. bonds when they are saving funds for a child's college education or for retirement.

Do you live in a state with high income taxes? One of the attractions in purchasing a U.S. Treasury Bond, Bill or Note is that the interest is not taxable in your state or municipality. Yes, you will have to pay federal income tax on your profit, but not state or local income taxes.

Most people consider the investment in these U.S. government securities (as Bonds, Notes and Bills are known) to be fully safe, as they are backed by the federal government which is more likely to be able to repay you than any company. Unlike a corporation which can go bankrupt, it is generally believed that if you invest in U.S. securities you will receive interest and get your full investment back when the security matures.

In a recession, U.S. government bonds are an ideal investment because they are known for outperforming stocks during tough economic times.
But like anything else in the world, there has to be a down-side. Like all bonds and stocks, U.S. government securities have some risks too. First, the interest rate rising can be a problem for your bond. If prices in the general marketplace go up and you need cash,

you will sell your U.S. Treasury bond before it is mature. Based on the interest rate at the time, it could be worth more or less than its value. If you bought the U.S. securities when interest rates were going up, then chances are you are going to get less than its value. But if you bought bonds when interest rates were low, then you are probably going to make a nice profit.

Another concern to have with U.S. government securities is the inflation risk. If inflation rises while you own the bonds, then the value of your bond may decline, in terms of what it is worth to you.

31

From Rags to Riches

Many of today's rich were able to acquire their wealth by taking advantage of opportunities during tough economic times. Often they readjusted their skills, used their creative streak, and kept their eyes and ears open for ways to make money. The stories of how they moved from "rags to riches," from poverty to millionaire, are real and have happened to people you know. Oprah Winfrey. Martha Stewart. J.K. Rowling. Jim Carrey. These are among the best known examples.

Oprah used her talent to get a job and climb the ladder in the TV world. She overcame being raped as a young girl and giving birth to a stillborn in her teens, and was determined to create a better life for herself. Martha Stewart looked beyond her family's meager finances, learned her way around the stock market, became a stock broker, and then took her financial success to other industries. When Jim Carrey sought a way out of the family's poverty, he realized that he did not have skills or a strong educational background, but he did have a talent for comedy. As a teenager, he left a job in a tire factory, worked hard in local comedy clubs, and ultimately became one of Hollywood's wealthiest comedians. J.K. Rowling was a single mother, living on welfare, who explored her creativity to create Harry Potter. She came up with the idea once while on public transportation and refused to accept "no" for an answer when several publishing houses rejected her story idea. Her persistence paid off when one publishing house took a chance on her and made her a millionaire.

The one common thread is that it didn't happen overnight for any of them. They were extremely poor and they worked hard and made their way to the top. Most people who become overnight millionaires, such as through the lottery, lose all their money within a few years. It is usually those who take the slower route of working hard and being creative who establish a strong financial foundation, and often accumulate real wealth, which can be passed on for generations. Remember that when these now-famous individuals were starting out, no one knew their names. And it can happen to you. Using some of the ideas in this book, you can overcome financial difficulties and find your success, like the individuals portrayed in this chapter.

Earl Tupper

During the Great Depression, while millions were suffering in poverty, some utilized the situation to find ways to profit. One individual who used the downtime of the Great Depression to explore his talents and successfully increased his financial status is Earl Tupper, of the famed Tupperware company. He was born to a poor farming family but he always had hopes of becoming a millionaire, and he successfully worked towards that goal.

Because he grew up in a poor home and wanted to have a very different life for himself, Earl always looked for opportunities to make money. He was always using his hands, inventing products and coming up with innovative ideas. While he was tinkering with his interests, he knew that he had to have an income and he set up a landscaping business. But during the Depression, his clients could not afford to spend money on gardening and pretty lawns, and he went into bankruptcy. Trying to bounce back while supporting his family, he considered himself fortunate to land a job in a plastics factory.

As the Depression continued and he needed a dependable income, Earl Tupper learned all he could about plastics and was determined to succeed there. He started to play around with plastics, and invested some of his hard-earned money to buy second-hand molding machines; with that, he made plastic containers to hold cigarettes and soap.

When the Depression ended, he used his knowledge and tinkered a little more until he developed the first products of what is today known as Tupperware. He worked hard and built the company slowly, but ultimately his dream came true, because he sought opportunities, was creative, and utilized his own talents to make it.

Andrew Carnegie

One of the best known rags to riches stories is that of Andrew Carnegie, in the second half of the nineteenth century. Andrew was born into a working class family, but when the Industrial Era hit Europe and machines replaced man, his father lost his job. The family faced poverty as the economic situation worsened, and they followed many others to America in hope of a better life.

Andrew was only 13 when he started working, and he put in hours like an adult. In an era when child labor was acceptable, he was working in a cotton mill 12 hours a day, 6 days a week. He switched to a job as a telegraph messenger, where he worked hard and slowly inched his way up the corporate ladder.

Andrew was smart and put aside, turning to someone more knowledgable to help him invest the money into businesses. It paid off. As he increased his profits from those investments, he re-invested the money, spreading it around into various places so as not to risk it all should one investment go sour. And although he was making money from his investments, he still continued to work hard and bring in a salary, not relying on his side efforts.

Among his investments, Andrew put money into the steel industry, which was growing dramatically at that time. As that became more profitable, he began to spend more time learning his way around that industry, and he subsequently created one of the largest steel companies in America.

Where did the poor boy from Scotland end up? In 2007, his company was bought out for the equivalent of 120 billion dollars.

Chris Gardner

Chris Gardner is not a household name, but many saw the 2006 movie of his life, "Pursuit of Happyness," in which he was portrayed by actor Will Smith.

Like many others who rose from poverty to wealth, Chris came from a broken home. His father abandoned the family; after his mother remarried, his step-father treated them so poorly that Chris fled the home and ended up in the U.S. Navy. Upon discharge, he entered the medical supplies industry where he saw some initial success, but as technology and medicine began to improve, he realized he would be needing to find himself a new job.

As his career collapsed, his wife left him. As a single father raising his child, Chris didn't know where to start, but he knew he wanted to be financially independent and comfortable. He was a good salesman, but he knew that wasn't enough. Walking down the street one day, he saw a man get out of an expensive car. Chris approached him and asked what he did for a living; what kind of job could buy a Ferrari? When

Chris learned that the man was a stockbroker, Chris decided he had found his new career.

It wasn't easy and it didn't happen quickly, but Chris was patient, learned what he had to do, and took the right steps. While studying for the licensing exam to become a stock broker, Chris and his son were homeless and even slept in a subway station when there wasn't enough room in the homeless shelter. He passed the exam, earned his way into a job at one of the leading financial investment companies, and worked very hard to prove that they made the right decision in hiring him. He swallowed his pride and made cold calls, worked long hours, and started to earn money.

After a number of years, Chris was earning enough to put money aside and he opened his own stock-brockerage firm.

Gurbaksh Chahal

Sure, you probably never heard of him. But he's a classic story that inspires people like you and I.

Gurbaksh, known by friends and colleagues as "G", made his money in technology. Unlike Bill Gates, who had successful relatives and went to Harvard, Gurbaksh was a high school drop-out. His parents immigrated to the United States from India with just $25 in their wallet when Gurbaksh was 4 years old. Two decades later, after much hard work and creativity, Gurbaksh made a name for himself when he sold his business to Yahoo! for $300 million.

When asked why he was successful in becoming a millionaire, Gurbaksh notes that he didn't follow the traditional path that had been laid out for him, but worked hard once he had chosen different steps for himself. He notes that most Indian immigrants to America become engineers or doctors. He decided to take a risk, believing that you can't be afraid to try new things, and if you are successful, the payoff is much greater. He looked around him to see what had potential, and learned that Internet advertising was taking off. Lucky for him, he decided to go down that career path. He learned the industry, built companies and sold them to make himself a millionaire.

Chris Roberts-Antieau

Her bio calls her a "true rags-to-riches story", and today she is one of the foremost fabric artists in America, with work featured in museums and collected by The White House, Oprah Winfrey, and even the Boxing Hall of Fame.

It started off slowly. A misfit in high school, Chris' creative side led her to art school, but she dropped out on the first day when she walked out of an art class and never went back. Art went to the back-burner on the professional level for a number of years. She was a mother at home with her 4 year old when she entered the work force, hand-making her own art and hitting the road to sell it at trade shows.

Her art is based on fabric pictures that she creates by cutting the fabric into shapes and sewing them onto a fabric background, which is then put into a frame that she hand-paints. She taught herself everything she needs to know, and incorporates her creativity and strong work ethic to make her business successful. She doesn't use fancy materials, but instead buys pieces of fabric at local stores and second-hand shops. While initially she was the sole employee of the business, today she has staff working for her and her products are picked up by major stores and art dealers.

But Chris doesn't take it for granted. She was raised "by parents who told me that anything is possible", and Chris acknowledges that things don't come easy. In her own words, "I work hard. I love what I do. I believe that we are here for a purpose. I am humbled by the blessing in my life."

Conrad Hilton

Conrad Hilton had many ups and downs in life, like most people who earn their wealth. When his father's business failed and he needed a career, Conrad moved to Texas hoping to start a new life. He tried his hand at opening a bank, but it failed. Without a place to live, he temporarily stayed in a hotel and he realized the potential that the industry had. He put together money and bought a hotel, paying attention to what didn't work at other hotels, and then using his resources to make his hotel better than those. Like Andrew Carnegie, once he started to earn money, he invested it into businesses. As his success increased, he began buying other hotels and ultimately building his own. He set a specific goal of managing his money and investments property so that he could add a new hotel to his ownership every year, and he worked hard to try and achieve that.

He was very successful but then the Great Depression hit and his hotels were not longer busy. He started losing money and fell into debt. He subsequently encountered personal problems and got divorced. It took several years of living in debt before he was able to put together money to invest – once again – in the hotel industry. His patience and hard work paid off, turning into the success of the Hilton Hotel chain.

Each of these stories has one thing in common. Every successful person has experienced setbacks along the way but had the courage to get up and try again. Every "rags to riches" story features people who believed in themselves when the chips were down and it seemed that nothing was in their favor, but they turned their luck around through grit and determination. If you have not already read my chapter "How to Manifest Money and Success", it can show you the way to turn your luck around and write your own "rags to riches" story.

32

Recession Pitfalls
to Avoid

One of the common mistakes people make during difficult economic times is to take action that they think will protect their money or save them costs, but these cannot be the only steps you take. For example, many people who lived through eras in which banks failed (Great Depression, the Savings & Loan collapse in the 1980s, etc.) are scared to keep their money in a bank. Instead of securing funds in a savings account that allows them to earn interest and also provides security for their funds, they keep it stored at home (even under mattresses) where it is susceptible to theft.

Another mistake that is often made is cutting back or scrimping on areas that they should not. Yes, it is true that a penny saved is a penny earned. But you have to know where to save your pennies. For example, if your refrigerator broke and you didn't know how to fix it, you would call a repairman because you need a refrigerator to live. But you think you can fix other things by yourself, or avoid putting money towards areas that you should. Each family has to evaluate the value of "extras", but be knowledgesable before you make decisions and then make the decisions wisely.

If you follow some of the ideas in this book (because obviously you won't be able to do everything), you should be on the road to financial stability and success. But some of the steps you need to take will require you to make priorities with your financial calculations, and this chapter helps identify some of them.

Pay your debts

The first thing to do when money starts to become tight is to make sure you prioritize paying your debts. Usually there are added fees for unpaid bills, such as interest. In the long run, you get yourself into further debt. Moreover, when times are tough, debt-holders will be quick to take legal action to recoup debt, so in addition to interest and late fees that may accrue, you can end up having to hire a lawyer and fight a legal batter.

Paying debts will also help keep your credit rating good, which is important for the long-term as well. If you have a lower income coming in now, you can always try to negotiate better repayment terms so that you can keep up with your payments while turning in less money. And if you lost your job, sometimes you can get a deferment on paying until you have a steady income.

Do you own a car?

Maybe you don't really need one (or two)…but maybe you do. Ho do you know when you should keep a car during lean times? It comes down to two key things: need and practicality.

If you are working from home and don't have to venture out much for meetings, then you may be able to save more by selling your car. And if you don't work from home, perhaps you live in an area with good pulic transportation. Determine how much you use your car, and how much it would inconvenience your family not to have one.

Don't make the mistake of selling your car for the income. Usually you won't earn enough to justify the taxicabs, trains or buses you will have to start taking if you depend on your car every day. But what you should review is how much you are spending on insurance, gas and upkeep. Is that the best use of your money? Keep in mind that if you own a car, you can't scrimp on insurance, gas or general upkeep. If a tire goes flat, you have to have it repaired.

Owning a car means you have to have the money to support it, and that it really is the best use of your funds at this time. That is a decision only you (and your family) can make.

It pays to have good professionals

When you prioritize your funding, don't forget to include good professional advisors. Many people have an accountant or lawyer or financial advisor. They cost money, and this is not an area to cut back unnecessarily.

Yes, you may be able to learn how to do your own taxes. But chances are your accountant will know more than you will about different loopholes, changes in the law, and way to save money through taxes. You may save the initial fees of paying someone to do your tax returns, but in the long run you may pay higher taxes, the cost of fighting an audit from the IRS, or other costs that you are saving on now.

Likewise with an attorney. If you are opening your own business or facing legal problems, protect yourself with a good attorney. Or if you have a small business and need good contracts, don't depend on some of the free offerings on the Internet. If you are closing on a new house, don't share a lawyer with the other side to save on money. There are simply times that you need to make sure you have someone who is prioritizing your interests, which can ultimately save you money.

Investing your finances? Don't underestimate the value of a good financial advisor or stock broker.

Whatever your needs for professional help, this is not an area cut back without careful evaluation.

Don't forget yourself

When times are tough, people stop putting money into savings and pension plans. If you have a job now, as hard as it may seem to save, don't understimate the value a pension plan can have for you down the road. And in terms of savings, just because it seems terrible now doesn't mean that the worst has hit. Thinking positive is important, but you should make sure to have money put aside for an even rainier day.

At the same time, the stress of economic crises coupled with the cut-backs and potential increased demands at work (fewer employees but the same workload) can have an emotional impact. Your monthly budget should also include a little money – even just $5 – set aside for you. If you are married, make sure that you have separate "personal" money from your husband. It is very important to make sure that every now and then you treat yourself to something that makes you happy which often is not the same as your spouse. For a woman it could be cosmetics to feel good or a manicure once a month. For a man it could be a beer out with buddies. When times are tough, many people get very overwhelmed, and even depressed. A little pick-me-up every now and then is good. If you budget a little each month, you could buy something small every few weeks or save it and buy something bigger to treat yourself.

And don't forget to put aside some small money for special celebrations – whether it is an anniversary or birthday. You don't have to spend much – it could just mean splurging on icing for a cake you are making. But that little gesture can have a tremendous impact.

33

Conclusion

Despite the gloomy economic forecasts and negative business news bulletins we are hearing every day, we still believe there are reasons to be cheerful. Even during a recession there are exciting opportunities for individuals who have the courage to seize them. It takes more guts, but it is possible to get rich in tough times.

When writing this book, I specifically chose to give you a broad range of examples of the many different directions you could choose to take. This book shows that it IS possible to get rich in tough times, by following any of the routes that seems right for you and your family.

Remember, when severe economic challenges confront our communities and our country, as they do today, it is important to think "outside the box." Be creative with your skills, be flexible with your attitude, and be serious about finding a way to turn the bad times into good times.

I hope that I was able to convey how realistic you must be. If you have been laid off of work, you may not find the exact same job with the same benefits and salary at another company. But that shouldn't be your goal today. Right now, the focus must be on prospering despite the recession… with a positive attitude. This is a great opportunity to learn a new skill, try that home business you've been thinking about, cut back your unnecessary expenditures, and re-connect with old friends and colleagues as you network for job opportunities or other financial gains.

Yes, there is a pot of gold at the end of the rainbow; if you are determined to support yourself (and your family), I hope that the steps and suggestions I have outlined in these pages will bring you closer to financial success.